The Database Relational Model

A Retrospective Review and Analysis

A *historical account and assessment of
E. F. Codd's contribution
to the field of database technology*

C. J. Date

ADDISON-WESLEY

An imprint of Addison Wesley Longman, Inc.

*Reading, Massachusetts • Harlow, England • Menlo Park, California
Berkeley, California • Don Mills, Ontario • Sydney
Bonn • Amsterdam • Tokyo • Mexico City*

Thirty Years of Relational articles were originally published in print and online by Intelligent Enterprise, Miller Freeman Inc. Copyright held by the author and Intelligent Enterprise.

Library of Congress Cataloging-in-Publication Data

Date, C. J.
   The database relational model : a retrospective review and analysis / C. J. Date.
      p. cm.
   ISBN 0-201-61294-1
   1. Relational databases.   I. Title.

   QA76.9.D3 D368 2001
   005.75′6—dc21

                                                      00-026609

ISBN 0-201-61294-1

1 2 3 4 5 6 7 8 9 10—CRW—04 03 02 01 00
First printing, April 2000

To Ted, obviously

Contents

Preface

This book consists in essence of a series of twelve articles, originally published in the print and online portions of the Miller Freeman magazine *Intelligent Enterprise (Vol. 1*, Nos. 1–3, and *Vol. 2*, Nos. 1–9, October 1998 onward, copyright C. J. Date and *Intelligent Enterprise).* The overall title for the series was "30 Years of Relational," on the grounds that the articles were written, in part, to celebrate the relational model's 30th birthday. Their intent was—as it says on the title page of this book, more or less—to serve as a historical account and impartial analysis of E. F. Codd's (huge!) contribution to the field of database technology. Codd's relational model, represented by a startlingly novel series of research papers appearing over the period 1969-1979, was a revolution at the time, albeit one that was desperately needed. Now, however, it seems that—despite the fact that the entire multibillion dollar database industry is founded on Codd's original ideas— those ideas are in danger of being ignored or forgotten (or, at best, being paid mere lip service to). Certainly we can observe many examples today of those ideas being flouted in (among other things) database products, database designs, and database applications. It thus seems appropriate to take another look at Codd's original papers, with a view to assessing their true significance and restating (and reinforcing) their message for a new generation of database professionals.

I would like to thank Miller Freeman Inc. for permission to republish these articles here.

C. J. Date
Healdsburg, California
2000

Chapter 1

The Birth of the Relational Model

Part 1 of 3

Looking back at Codd's first two relational papers

It was thirty years ago today
Dr. Edgar showed the world the way . . .
—with apologies to Lennon & McCartney

Excuse the poetic (?) license, but it *was* thirty years ago, near enough, that Dr. Edgar F. Codd began work on what would become **The Relational Model of Data**. In 1969, he published the first in a brilliant series of highly original papers describing that work—papers that changed the world as we know it. Since that time, of course, many people have made contributions (some of them quite major) to database research in general and relational database research in particular, but none of those later contributions has been as significant or as fundamental as Codd's original work. A hundred years from now, I'm quite sure, database systems will still be based on Codd's relational foundation.

THE FIRST TWO PAPERS

As already mentioned, Codd's first relational paper, "Derivability, Redundancy, and Consistency of Relations Stored in Large Data Banks" [7], was published in 1969. Unfortunately, however, that paper was an IBM Research Report; as such, it carried a Limited Distribution Notice and therefore wasn't seen by as many people as it might have been (indeed, it's since become something of a collector's item). But the following year a revised version of that first paper was published in *Communications of the ACM* [9], and *that* version was much more widely disseminated and received much more attention, in the academic community at least. Indeed, that 1970 version, "A Relational Model of Data for Large Shared Data Banks," is usually credited with being the seminal paper in the field, though that characterization is perhaps a little unfair to its 1969 predecessor.

Note: As a matter of fact, the 1970 paper was subsequently republished in the Silver Anniversary issue of *Communications of the ACM* as one of a very select list of papers labeled "Milestones of Research." Other such "milestones" included:

- Edsger W. Dijkstra's paper on the THE operating system and his first paper on concurrency control;
- C. A. R. Hoare's papers on communicating sequential processes and an axiomatic basis for computer programming;
- Niklaus Wirth's paper on program development by stepwise refinement;

- Dennis M. Ritchie and Ken Thompson's paper on UNIX;

- R. L. Rivest, A. Shamir, and L. Adleman's paper on public-key encryption;

and other papers of similar stature.

Anyway, those first two papers of Codd's are certainly unusual in one respect: They stand up very well to being read—and indeed repeatedly *re*read—over 30 years later! (How many papers can you say *that* of?) At the same time, it has to be said too that they're not particularly *easy* to read, nor to understand . . . The writing is terse and a little dry, the style theoretical and academic, the notation and examples mostly rather mathematical in tone. As a consequence, I'm sure I'm right in saying that, to this day, only a tiny percentage of database professionals have actually read them. So I thought it would be interesting, and (I also thought) useful, to devote a short series of articles to a careful, unbiased, retrospective review and assessment of Codd's first two papers.

As I started to get involved in writing that review, however, I began to realize that it would be better not to limit myself to just the first two papers, but rather to take a look at *all* of Codd's early relational publications. What I plan to do, therefore, is consider the following important papers of Codd's in addition to the two already mentioned:

- A Data Base Sublanguage Founded on the Relational Calculus [11]

- Further Normalization of the Data Base Relational Model [12]

- Relational Completeness of Data Base Sublanguages [15]
- Interactive Support for Nonprogrammers: The Relational and Network Approaches [17]
- Extending the Database Relational Model to Capture More Meaning [19]

I'll also briefly touch on a few other papers from time to time. *Note:* It's worth mentioning that, unfortunately, several of the papers I'll be talking about were published in some pretty obscure places, with the result that they can be quite hard to track down nowadays. It would be nice if they could all be brought together and republished in book form someday (hint, hint).

One last preliminary remark: As I've written elsewhere [38], I don't mean to suggest that Codd's early papers got every last detail exactly right, or that Codd himself foresaw every last implication of his ideas. Indeed, it would be quite surprising if matters were otherwise! Minor mistakes and some degree of confusion are normal and natural when a major invention first sees the light of day; think of the telephone, or the automobile, or television (or even computers themselves, come to that—do you remember the prediction that three computers would be sufficient to serve all of the computing needs of the United States?). Be that as it may, I will, of course, be liberally applying the "20:20 hindsight" principle in what follows. Indeed, I think it's interesting to see how certain aspects of the relational model have evolved over time.

CODD'S FUNDAMENTAL CONTRIBUTIONS

For purposes of future reference, let me briefly summarize Codd's major contributions here. (I limit myself to relational contributions only! It's not as widely known as it ought to be, but the fact is that Codd deserves recognition for original work in at least two other areas as well—namely, *multiprogramming* [6] and *natural language processing* [16]. Details of those other contributions are beyond the scope of this series of articles, however.)

- Probably his biggest overall achievement was to make database management into a *science;* he put the field on to a solid scientific footing, by providing a theoretical framework—i.e., the relational model—within which a variety of important problems could be attacked in a scientific manner. In other words, the relational model really serves as the basis for a **theory** of data. (Indeed, the term "relational theory" is preferable in some ways to the term "relational model," and it might have been nice if Codd had used it. But he didn't.)

- As a consequence of the previous point, he introduced a welcome and sorely needed note of clarity and rigor into the database field.

- He introduced not only the relational model in particular, but the whole idea of a data model in general.

- He stressed the importance of the distinction (regrettably still widely misunderstood) between model and implementation.

- He saw the potential of using the ideas of predicate logic as a foundation for database management.

- He defined both a relational algebra and a relational calculus as a basis for dealing with data in relational form.

- He defined (albeit only informally) what was probably the first relational language, "Data Sublanguage ALPHA."

- He introduced the concept of functional dependence and defined the first three normal forms (1NF, 2NF, 3NF).

- He defined the key notion of *essentiality*.

THE 1969 PAPER

Now I want to focus on the 1969 paper specifically (though I will also mention points where the thinking in the 1970 paper seems to augment or supersede that of the 1969 version). The 1969 paper—which was, I remind you, entitled "Derivability, Redundancy, and Consistency of Relations Stored in Large Data Banks"—contains an introduction and the following six sections:

1. A Relational View of Data
2. Some Linguistic Aspects
3. Operations on Relations
4. Expressible, Named, and Stored Relations
5. Derivability, Redundancy, and Consistency
6. Data Bank Control

The paper's focus is worthy of note. As both the title and the abstract suggest, that focus is not so much on the relational model *per se* as it is on the provision of a means of investigating, in a precise and scientific manner, certain notions of *data redundancy* and *consistency*. Indeed, the term "the relational model," as such, doesn't occur in the paper at all!—though the introduction does speak of "a relational view . . . (or model) of data." The introduction also points out that the relational "view" enjoys several advantages over "the graph (or network) model presently in vogue," the following among them:

- It provides a means of describing data in terms of its natural structure only (that is, all details having to do with machine representation are excluded).

- It provides a basis for constructing a high-level retrieval language with "maximal [*sic*] data independence" (that is, independence between application programs and machine data representation—what we would now call, more specifically, *physical* data independence). Note the term "*retrieval* language," by the way; the 1970 paper replaced it by the term "*data* language," but the emphasis throughout both of the first two papers was always very heavily on query rather than update.

- It permits a clear evaluation of the scope and limitations of existing database systems.

- It also permits a clear evaluation of the relative merits of "competing data representations within a single system" (in other words, it provides a basis for an attack on the logical database design problem).

Note the numerous hints here of interesting developments to come! Anyway, let's move on to examine the sections of the paper one by one.

A Relational View of Data

Essentially, this section is concerned with what later came to be called the *structural* part of the relational model; that is, it discusses relations *per se* (and briefly mentions keys), but it doesn't get into the relational operations at all (what later came to be called the *manipulative* part of the model).

The paper's definition of the term "relation" is worth examining briefly. That definition runs more or less as follows:

- Given sets *S1, S2, . . . , Sn* (not necessarily distinct), *R* is a *relation* on those *n* sets if it is a set of *n*-tuples [or *rows*] each of which has its first element from *S1*, its second element from *S2,* and so on. We shall refer to *Sj* as the *j*th *domain* of *R* . . . *R* is said to have *degree n.* (And the 1970 paper adds: More concisely, *R* is a subset of the Cartesian product of its domains.)

Although (of course) mathematically respectable, this definition can be criticized from a database standpoint—here comes the 20:20 hindsight!—on a couple of counts:

- It doesn't clearly distinguish between *domains* on the one hand and *attributes,* or *columns,* on the other. It's true that the paper does introduce the term *attribute* later, but it doesn't define it formally and it doesn't use it consistently. (The 1970 paper does introduce the term *active domain* to mean the set of values from a given domain actually appearing in the database at any given time, but that concept isn't the same as "attribute" either.) As a result, there has been much confusion in the industry over the distinction between domains and attributes, and such confusions persist to the present day. (In fairness, I should add that the first—i.e., 1975—edition of my book *An Introduction to Database Systems* [49] was also not very clear on the domain *vs.* attribute distinction.)

As a matter of fact, the 1969 paper later gives an example that, at least from an intuitive standpoint, stumbles over this very confusion. The example involves a relation called PART with (among others) two columns called QUANTITY_ON_HAND and QUANTITY_ON_ORDER. It seems to me likely in practice that these two columns would both be defined on the same domain, but the example clearly says they're not (it refers to them as distinct *domains,* and then says those domains "correspond to what are commonly called . . . *attributes*").

- Note too that the definition specifies that the domains (and therefore attributes) of a relation have an *ordering,* left to right. The 1970 paper does say that users shouldn't have to deal with "domain-ordered relations" as such but rather with "their domain-unordered counterparts" (which it calls *relationships*), but that refinement seems to have escaped the attention of certain members of the database community—including, very unfortunately, the designers of the language SQL, in which the columns of a table definitely do have a left-to-right ordering.

Codd then goes on to define a "data bank" (which we would now more usually call a *database,* of course) to be "a collection of time-varying relations . . . of assorted degrees," and states that "each [such] relation may be subject to insertion of additional n-tuples, deletion of existing ones, and alteration of components of any of its existing n-tuples." Here, unfortunately, we run smack into the historical confusion between relation **values** and relation **variables** (or *relvars,* as *The Third Manifesto* calls them [52]). In mathematics (and indeed in Codd's own definition, already quoted), a relation is simply a *value,* and there's just no way it can vary over time; that is, there's no such thing as a "time-varying relation." But we can certainly have *variables—relation* variables, that is—whose values are relation values (different relation values at different times), and that's really what Codd's "time-varying relations" are.

A failure to distinguish adequately between these two distinct concepts has been another rich source of subsequent confusion. For this reason, I would have preferred to couch the discussions in the remainder of this series in terms of relation values and relation variables explicitly, rather than in terms of just relations (time-varying or otherwise). Unfortunately, however, such an approach turned out to involve too much rewriting and (worse) restructuring of the material I needed to quote and examine from Codd's own papers, and so I decided, reluctantly, to drop the idea. I seriously hope no further confusions arise from that decision!

Back to the 1969 paper. The next concept introduced is the crucial one—very familiar now, of course—of a *key* (i.e., a unique identifier). A key is said to be *nonredundant* if every attribute it contains is necessary for the purpose of unique identification; that is, if any attribute were removed, what would be left wouldn't be a unique identifier any more. ("Key" here thus means what we now call a *superkey,* and a "nonredundant" key is what we now call a *candidate* key—candidate keys being "nonredundant," or *irreducible,* by definition.)

Incidentally, the 1970 paper uses the term *primary* key in place of just *key.* Observe therefore that "primary key" in the 1970 paper does *not* mean what the term is usually taken to mean nowadays, because (a) it doesn't have to be nonredundant, and (b) a given relation can have any number of such keys. However, the paper does go on to say that if a given relation "has two or more nonredundant primary keys, one of them is arbitrarily selected and called *the* primary key."

The 1970 paper also introduces the term *foreign key.* (Actually, the 1969 paper briefly mentions the concept too, but it doesn't use the term.) However, the definition is unnecessarily restrictive, in that—for some reason—it doesn't permit a primary key (or candidate key? or superkey?) to be a foreign key. The relational model as now understood includes no such restriction, of course.

In connection with the foreign key concept, incidentally, the 1970 paper also has this to say:

In previous work there has been a strong tendency to treat the data in a data bank as consisting of two parts, one part consisting of [entities] . . . and the other . . . of [relationships] between the various entities . . . This distinction is difficult to maintain when one may have foreign keys in any relation whatsoever . . . [At the logical level,] there appears to be no advantage in making such a distinction (there may be some advantage, however, [at the physical level]).

In other words, there's really no justification for making a formal distinction between "entities" and "relationships" at the logical level.

Well, that's all I have room for in this chapter. At least I've laid some groundwork for what's to come, but Codd's contributions are so many and varied that there's no way they can be dealt with adequately in just one or two articles. It's going to be a fairly lengthy journey.

It was thirty years ago today
Dr. Edgar showed the world the way
His relations won't go out of style
They're guaranteed to last a while
So may I introduce to you
The act you've known for all these years
Dr. Edgar's Data Model Band!

Chapter 2

The Birth of the Relational Model

Part 2 of 3

*Continuing our look at Codd's first
two relational papers*

In Chapter 1, I began my retrospective review of Codd's first two relational papers [7,9]. In particular, I took a detailed look at the first section ("A Relational View of Data") of the first paper [7]. Just to remind you, that paper had six sections overall:

1. A Relational View of Data
2. Some Linguistic Aspects
3. Operations on Relations
4. Expressible, Named, and Stored Relations
5. Derivability, Redundancy, and Consistency
6. Data Bank Control

THE 1969 PAPER CONTINUED

Some Linguistic Aspects

Codd opened this section with the following crucial observation: "The adoption of a relational view of data . . . permits the development of a universal retrieval sublanguage based on the second-order predicate calculus." (Note that "second-order," by the way; the 1969 paper explicitly permitted relations to be defined on domains having relations as elements. I'll come back to this point in the next chapter, when I discuss the 1970 paper in detail.)

It was Codd's very great insight that a database could be thought of as a set of relations, that a relation in turn could be thought of as a set of propositions (assumed by convention to be *true*), and hence that all of the apparatus of formal logic could be directly applied to the problem of database access and related problems. In this section of the paper, he sketched the salient features of an access language based on such logical concepts. The following points are worthy of note:

- The language would be set-level.
- The emphasis would be on data retrieval (though update operations would of course be included too).
- The language would not be computationally complete —it was meant to be a "sublanguage," to be "[embedded] in a variety of host languages . . . Any [computational] functions needed can be defined in [the host language] and invoked [from the sublanguage]."

   Personally, I've never been entirely convinced that factoring out data access into a separate "sublanguage" was a good idea (see, e.g. reference [26]), but it's certainly been with us, in the shape of *embedded SQL,* for a good while now. In this connection, incidentally, it's interesting to note that with the addition in 1996 of the PSM feature ("Persistent Stored Modules") to the SQL standard, SQL has now become a computationally complete language in its own right!—meaning that a host language as such is no longer logically necessary (with SQL, that is).

■ "Some deletions may be triggered by others, if deletion dependencies . . . are declared." In other words, Codd already had in mind, in 1969, the possibility of triggered "referential actions" such as CASCADE DELETE (and in the 1970 paper he extended this notion to include UPDATE referential actions as well).

■ The language would provide *symmetric exploitation.* That is, the user would be able to access a given relation using any combination of its attributes as *knowns* and the remaining ones as *unknowns.* "This is a system feature [that is] missing from many current information systems." Quite so!—but of course we take it as a *sine qua non* now, at least in the relational world (the object world doesn't seem to think it's so important, for some reason).

Operations on Relations

This section of the paper provides definitions of certain relational operations (summarized below); in other words, it describes what later came to be called the *manipulative* part of the relational model. Before getting into the definitions, however, Codd states: "Most users would not be directly concerned with these operations. *Information systems designers and people concerned with data bank control should, however, be thoroughly familiar with [them]*" (my italics). How true! In my experience, regrettably, people who *should* be thoroughly familiar with these operations are all too often not so. But I digress . . .

The operations defined are *permutation, projection, join, tie,* and *composition* (the 1970 paper added *restriction,* which I'll cover here too for convenience). It's interesting to note that the definitions for *restriction* and *join* are rather different from those usually given today, also that two of the operations, *tie* and *composition,* are now rarely considered.

Throughout what follows, the symbols $X, Y, \ldots$ (and so on) denote either individual attributes or combinations of attributes, as necessary.

Permutation: Reorder the attributes of a relation, left to right. (As noted in Chapter 1, relations in the 1969 paper had a left-to-right ordering to their attributes. By contrast, the 1970 paper states that permutation is intended purely for internal use, since of course the left-to-right ordering of attributes is—or should be—irrelevant so far as the user is concerned.)

Projection: More or less as understood today (though the syntax is different; in what follows, I'll use the syntax $R\{X\}$ to denote the projection of R over X). *Note:* The name "projection" derives from the fact that a relation of degree

n can be regarded as representing points in n-dimensional space, and projecting that relation over m of its attributes ($m \le n$) can be seen as projecting those points on to the corresponding m axes.

Join: See below.

Tie: Given a relation $A\{X1,X2,...,Xn\}$, the *tie* of A is the restriction of A to just those rows in which $A.Xn = A.X1$ (using "restriction" in its modern sense, not in the special sense defined below).

Composition: Given relations $A\{X,Y\}$ and $B\{Y,Z\}$, the composition of A with B is the projection on X and Z of a join of A with B (the reason I say "a" join, not "the" join, is explained below). *Note:* The *natural* composition is the projection on X and Z of the *natural* join—again, see below.

Restriction: Given relations $A\{X,Y\}$ and $B\{Y\}$, the restriction of A by B is defined to be the maximal subset of A such that $A\{Y\}$ is a subset—not necessarily a proper subset—of B.

In addition to the above, Codd says "all of the usual set operations are [also] applicable . . . [but] the result may not be a relation." In other words, definitions of the specifically relational versions of *Cartesian product, union, intersection,* and *difference* still lay in the future at the time Codd was writing his 1969 paper.

Let's get back to **join**. Given relations $A\{X,Y\}$ and $B\{Y,Z\}$, the paper defines a *join* of A with B to be any relation $C\{X,Y,Z\}$ such that $C\{X,Y\} = A$ and $C\{Y,Z\} = B$. Note, therefore, that:

- A and B can be joined (or "are joinable") only if their projections on Y are identical!—that is, only if A and B both contain exactly the same set of Y values, a condition one might have thought unlikely to be satisfied in practice.

- If A and B are joinable, then many different joins can exist (in general). The well-known *natural* join—called the *linear* natural join in the paper, in order to distinguish it from another kind called a *cyclic* join—is an important special case, but it's not the only possibility (again in general).

Oddly, however, the definition given in the paper for the natural join operation doesn't actually require A and B to be "joinable" in the foregoing special sense! In fact, that definition is more or less the same as the one we use today.

Let me try to explain where that rather restrictive "joinability" notion comes from. Codd begins his discussion of joins by asking the important question: "Under what circumstances does the join of two relations preserve all of the information in those two relations?" And he shows that the property of "joinability" is sufficient to ensure that all information is thus preserved (because no row of either operand is lost in the join). Further, he also shows that if A and B are "joinable" and either $A.X$ is functionally dependent on $A.Y$ or $B.Z$ is functionally dependent on $B.Y$, then the natural join is the only join possible (though he doesn't actually use the functional dependence terminology—that also lay in the future). In other words, what Codd is doing here is laying some groundwork for the all-important theory of *nonloss decomposition* (which, of course, he was to elaborate in subsequent papers; I'll get to those papers in future chapters).

Note: Remarkably, Codd also gives an example that shows he was aware, back in 1969, of the fact that some relations can't be nonloss-decomposed into two projections but can be nonloss-decomposed into three! This example was apparently overlooked by most of the paper's original readers; at any rate, it seemed to come as a surprise to the research community when that same fact was rediscovered several years later—in 1977, to be precise [1]. Indeed, it was that rediscovery that led to Fagin's invention of the "ultimate" normal form, 5NF, also known as PJ/NF ("projection-join normal form") [53].

Expressible, Named, and Stored Relations

"Associated with a data bank are three collections of relations: the *expressible* set, the *named* set, and the *stored* set" (slightly paraphrased). To elaborate: An *expressible* relation is one that can be designated by means of an expression of the data access language (which is assumed to support the operations described in the previous section); a *named* relation is one that has a user-known name; and a *stored* relation is one that's directly represented in physical storage somehow.

I do have a small complaint here (with 20:20 hindsight once again). To be specific, it seems to me a little unfortunate that Codd used the term *stored relation* in the

way he did. Personally, I would have divided the expressible relations into two kinds, *base* relations and *derivable*
ones; I would have defined a derivable (or *derived*) relation to be an expressible relation whose value at all times
is derived according to some relational expression from
other expressible relations, and a base relation to be an
expressible relation that's not derivable in this sense. In
other words, the base relations are the "given" ones, the
derivable ones are all of the others. And then I would
have made it very clear that base and stored relations
are not necessarily the same thing (see Fig. 2.1). As it is,
the paper effectively suggests—rather strongly, in fact—
that base and stored relations *are* the same thing (basically because it doesn't even bother to mention base
relations as a separate category at all).

Now, it's certainly true that base relations are essentially the same as stored relations in most SQL products
today. In other words, it's certainly true that most people
think of base relations as mapping very directly to physical storage (in those products). But there's no *logical* requirement for that mapping to be so simple!—indeed, the

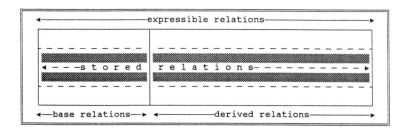

Fig. 2.1   Kinds of relations

fact that there's supposed to be a clear distinction between model and implementation dictates that we say *nothing* about physical storage at all, in the model. To be more specific, the degree of variation allowed between base and stored relations should be *at least as great* as that allowed between derived and base relations; the only logical requirement is that it must be possible to *obtain* the base relations somehow from those that are physically stored (and then the derived ones can be obtained too).

As already indicated, however, most products today provide very little support for this idea; that is, most products today provide very much less data independence than relational technology is theoretically capable of. And as I've written elsewhere—see, e.g., reference [32]—this fact is precisely why we run into the notorious *denormalization* issue. Of course, denormalization is sometimes necessary (for performance reasons), but *it should be done at the physical storage level, **not** at the logical or base relation level.* Because most systems today essentially equate stored and base relations, however, there is much confusion over this simple point; furthermore, of course, denormalization usually has the side effect of corrupting an otherwise clean logical design, with well-known undesirable consequences.

Enough of this griping. Codd goes on to say:

- "If the traffic on some unnamed but expressible relation grows to significant proportions, then it should be given a name and thereby included in the named set" (somewhat paraphrased).

In other words, make it a *view!* So Codd was already talking about the idea of views as "canned queries," way back in 1969.

- "Decisions regarding which relations belong in the named set are based . . . on the logical needs of the community of users, and particularly on the ever-increasing investment in programs using relations by name as a result of past membership . . . in the named set."

Here Codd is saying that views are the mechanism for providing *logical data independence*—in particular, the mechanism for ensuring that old programs continue to run as the database evolves.

- "On the other hand, decisions regarding which relations belong in the stored set are based . . . on . . . performance requirements . . . and changes that take place in these [requirements]."

And here he's drawing *a very sharp distinction* between the logical and physical levels.

Derivability, Redundancy, and Consistency

In this section, Codd begins to address some of the issues that later came to be included in the *integrity* part of the relational model. A relation is said to be *derivable* if and only if it's "expressible" in the sense of the previous section. (Note, therefore, that this definition of derivability is not quite the same as the one I was advocating above, because—at least tacitly—it includes the base relations.) A set of relations is then said to be *strongly redundant* if it includes at least one relation that's derivable (in Codd's sense) from other relations in the set.

Note: The 1970 paper refines this definition slightly, as follows: A set of relations is said to be *strongly redundant* if it includes at least one relation that has a projection—possibly the *identity* projection, meaning the projection over all attributes—that's derivable from other relations in the set. (I've taken the liberty of simplifying Codd's definition somewhat, though of course I've tried to preserve his original intent.)

Codd then observes that the *named* relations probably will be strongly redundant in this sense, because they'll probably include both (a) base relations and (b) views that are derived from those base relations. (What the paper actually says is that "[such redundancy] may be employed to improve accessibility of certain kinds of information which happen to be in great demand"; this is one way of saying that views are a useful shorthand.) However, the *stored* relations will usually not be strongly redundant. Codd elaborates on this point in the 1970 paper:

- "If . . . strong redundancies in the named set are directly reflected . . . in the stored set . . . then, generally speaking, extra storage space and update time are consumed [though there might also be] a drop in query time for some queries and in load on the central processing units."

  Aside: Personally, I would have said the *base* relations should definitely not be strongly redundant, but the *stored* ones might be (depending—as always at the storage level—on performance considerations). *End of aside.*

Codd then goes on to say that, given a set of relations, the system should be informed of any redundancies that apply to that set, so that it can enforce *consistency;* the set will be consistent if it conforms to the stated redundancies and inconsistent otherwise, of course. I should point out, however, that this definition of consistency certainly doesn't capture all possible kinds of integrity, nor does the notion of strong redundancy capture all possible kinds of redundancy. As a simple counterexample, consider a database containing just one relation, say EMP {EMP#,DEMP#,BUDGET}, in which the following functional dependencies are satisfied:

```
EMP#  → DEPT#
DEPT# → BUDGET
```

This database certainly involves some redundancy, but it isn't "strongly" redundant according to the definition.

Note: I should explain why Codd uses the term *strong* redundancy. He does so to distinguish it from another kind, also defined in the paper, which he calls *weak* redundancy. I omit the details here, however, because—unlike just about every other concept introduced in the first two papers!—this particular notion doesn't seem to have led to anything very significant (in any case, the example given in the paper doesn't even conform to Codd's own definition). The interested reader is referred to the original paper for the specifics.

Data Bank Control

This, the final section of the 1969 paper, offers a few suggestions for what to do if inconsistencies are discovered. "The generation of an inconsistency . . . could be logged internally, so that if it were not remedied within some reasonable time . . . the system could notify the security officer [*sic*]. Alternatively, the system could [inform the user] that such and such relations now need to be changed to restore consistency . . . Ideally, [different system actions] should be possible . . . for different subcollections of relations." Here I would just comment—here comes the hindsight once again—that if as suggested earlier the database is to be regarded as a (correct!) logical system, it must *never* be allowed to contain any inconsistencies, at least from the user's point of view. In other words, "remedying inconsistencies" needs to be done on an individual statement-by-statement basis (not even on a transaction-by-transaction basis). See reference [52] for further elaboration of this point.

Chapter 3

The Birth of the Relational Model

Part 3 of 3

*Concluding our look at Codd's first
two relational papers*

In Chapter 2 I finished my retrospective review of the very first of Codd's relational papers [7]. Now I want to turn my attention to that paper's successor, "A Relational Model of Data for Large Shared Data Banks"—probably the most famous paper in the entire history of database management—which appeared the following year (1970) in *Communications of the ACM* [9]. As I said in Chapter 1, that second paper was mostly just a revision of the first, but it did also introduce a few additional concepts that are deserving of comment here.

THE 1970 PAPER

The 1970 paper consists of two principal parts, divided into sections as follows:

Compared to the 1969 paper, there are two major new sections, 1.2 and (especially) 1.4. In addition, the 1969 section "Derivability, Redundancy, and Consistency" has been split into two (2.2 and 2.3), and a summary has been added. In particular, note the shift in focus, as evidenced by the new title (and new abstract) and the new section 1.2. Specifically, whereas the 1969 paper stressed the notions of data redundancy and related matters, the new paper concentrates on the relational model *per se,* and especially on the usefulness of that model in providing *data independence* (meaning, primarily, *physical* data independence). Of course, it does also discuss all the other uses for, and advantages of, relations as mentioned in the 1969 paper.

However, easily the most significant change *vis-à-vis* the 1969 paper is the suggestion that all relations should be *normalized.* I'll discuss this change in detail in the section "Normal Form," later.

DATA DEPENDENCIES IN
EXISTING SYSTEMS

As just noted, the 1970 paper, much more than its 1969 predecessor, concerns itself with the question of data independence. In the abstract, Codd says: "Users of large data banks must be protected from having to know how the data is organized in the machine . . . Activities of users at terminals and most application programs should remain unaffected when the internal representation of data is changed." In other words, we want *physical data independence*. And he continues: "[Such activities and programs should also remain unaffected] even when some aspects of the external representation are changed"; in other words, we want *logical* data independence too.

Codd goes on to discuss various examples of the *lack* of data independence found in database systems at the time; specifically, he discusses *ordering, indexing,* and *access path* dependence. He then presents a simple example ilustrating such dependencies in systems that provide "tree-structured or slightly more general network models of the data" (in other words, hierarchic systems like IMS and network systems like IDS). *Note:* IDS was the forerunner of the better known system IDMS; Codd was writing before IDMS appeared on the scene.

It's worth taking a moment here to reflect on how far we've come! From the user's point of view, of course, the solution to the *ordering* dependence problem is (in SQL terms) the ORDER BY clause; that is, users should not be limited to predefined orderings, physical or otherwise, but should be able to request any ordering they like, dynamically. And if the user requests an ordering not directly represented in the stored version of the data, then the system should be able to sort or index the data dynamically.

Similarly, the solution to the *indexing* dependence problem is to exclude, ruthlessly, all references to indexes from applications. Instead, applications should be allowed to request access to data in any way they like, and some system component—what we would now call the *optimizer*—should take responsibility for deciding when and when not to use indexes in response to such requests. Separate CREATE INDEX and DROP INDEX statements should be available for use at any time, independent of what applications might currently exist and what their logical data access requirements might be.

Likewise, the solution to the *access path* dependence problem is to exclude all access paths from the user's view of the data (as is done in relational systems, of course, but was *not* done in systems like IMS and IDS). *Note:* Modern readers might find Codd's distinction between indexing and access path dependence a little puzzling; after all, an index is surely just a special case of an access path. What Codd had in mind, however, was the following: Data as seen by the user in a hierarchic or network system included certain constructs (sometimes called *links*) that— no matter how much their defenders might argue that they were really just *logical* access paths—invariably served as *physical* access paths as well. Thus, for example, if such an access path were removed, certain applications would cease to work.

NORMAL FORM

As already noted, easily the most significant change in the 1970 paper over the 1969 version is the idea that relations should always be *normalized;* that is, they should be defined on "domains whose elements are atomic (nondecomposable) values" only. Note carefully, therefore, that *normalized* here just means what we would now call *first normal form,* 1NF (the higher normal forms—2NF, 3NF, and so on—were defined later). Codd cites the following advantages of insisting on such normalization:

- A normalized relation "can be represented in storage by a two-dimensional column-homogeneous array . . . [whereas] some more complicated data structure is necessary for a relation [that is unnormalized]."

  It's curious that Codd chooses to focus on *simple representation in storage* as his first argument in favor of normalization!—but perhaps he really means *simple representation as far as the user is concerned.* Be that as it may, his use of the term *array* is also a little strange, given that array elements are usually accessed by means of positional addressing, while relation elements (*n*-tuples) are most certainly not. (Also, arrays usually contain a fixed number of elements, while relations do not.)

- The simplicity of the array representation is also claimed as an advantage "for communication of bulk data between systems which use widely different representations of the data. The communication form would be a suitably compressed version of the array representation and (a) would be devoid of pointers, (b) would avoid all dependence on hash addressing schemes, (c) would contain no indexes or ordering fields" (slightly paraphrased).

The second sentence here seems to be Codd's first explicit mention of the fact that the relational model expressly excludes pointers—a fact that subsequently became the subject of much debate (and regrettably still is), as I'm sure you know.

- "The adoption of a relational model of data . . . permits the development of a universal data sublanguage based on an applied predicate calculus. A first-order predicate calculus suffices if the collection of relations is in normal form."

Now *this* is an important point!—and it marks a major departure from the 1969 paper, which (as we saw in Chapter 2) talked in terms of *second*-order predicate calculus, not first. *Note:* For the benefit of readers who might not be familiar with these concepts, let me just say that (in relational terms) "first-order" means we can quantify over the *rows* of a relation, while "second-order" would mean we could quantify over *relations per se*. Thus, first-order logic allows us to formulate queries such as "Does supplier S1 exist in the suppliers relation?"; second-order logic would enable us to formulate queries such as "Does supplier S1 exist in *any* relation?"

I'd like to elaborate briefly on this question of normalization. I do agree with Codd that it's desirable to stay in the realm of first-order logic if possible. At the same time, however, I reject the idea of "atomic values"—at least in the sense that there might be any such thing as *absolute* atomicity. Thus, in *The Third Manifesto* [25,52], by Hugh Darwen and myself, we allow domains to contain *values of arbitrary complexity* (they—the values, that is—can even be relations); nevertheless, we do still stay within the confines of first-order logic. Further discussion of this issue would take us too far afield here; if you want to know more, you can find the details in another paper by Hugh [24].

Codd goes on in the 1970 paper to give a simple example showing what's involved in normalizing an unnormalized relation. As already noted, "normalizing" here just means getting to *first* normal form, and the example is therefore essentially straightforward. However, the paper does also include the following tantalizing remarks: "Further operations of a normalizing kind are possible. These are not discussed in this paper." Another hint of interesting developments to come!

Incidentally, Codd also remarks that "he knows of no application that would involve a primary key with a component defined on a domain whose elements are *not* atomic values" (considerably paraphrased). In fact, such applications do exist; one such is described in reference [24]. However, the existence of such applications doesn't mean that there exist relations that can't be normalized (the issue, again, is what exactly *atomicity* means). Again, however, further discussion would take us too far afield here.

MISCELLANEOUS ISSUES

I'll bring this review of Codd's 1970 paper to a close with a few miscellaneous points that don't fit neatly into any of the preceding sections.

- Regarding the business of using predicate logic, and in particular the quantifiers (EXISTS and FORALL) of that logic, in a data access language, Codd has this to say: "Because each relation in a practical data bank is a finite set at every instant of time, the existential and universal quantifiers can be expressed in terms of a function that counts the number of elements in any finite set." This is an interesting remark! It seems to me to be tantamount to admitting that we're not really dealing with predicate logic after all, but merely with *propositional* logic.

- The paper also includes the following brief remarks on *performance:* "[The] data system must provide a means of translating user requests . . . into . . . efficient . . . actions on the current stored representation. For a high level data language this presents a challenging design problem. Nevertheless, it is a problem which must be solved—as more users obtain concurrent access to a large data bank, responsibility for providing efficient response and throughput shifts from the . . . user to the data system." Prophetic words! Codd here is pointing out the necessity for an optimizer component in the DBMS, and tacitly suggesting that there might be some interesting research issues in this area.

- Another quote: "A lack of understanding of [the semantics of the relational operators] has led several
systems designers into what may be called the *connection trap.* [For example, suppose we have a nonrelational system in which] each supplier description is
linked by pointers to the descriptions of each part supplied by that supplier, and each part description is
similarly linked to the descriptions of each project
which uses that part. A conclusion is now drawn
which is, in general, erroneous: namely that, if all
possible paths are followed from a given supplier via
the [corresponding] parts . . . to the projects using
those parts, one will obtain a valid set of all projects
supplied by that supplier. Such a conclusion is correct
only in the very special case that the target relation
between projects and suppliers is, in fact, the *natural
composition* of the other two relations." *Note:* I discussed the natural composition operator in Chapter 2.

  Of course, we don't have to be following pointers in
order to fall into the connection trap—the very same
logical error can unfortunately be made in a purely relational system too. Indeed, some writers have criticized relational systems on exactly these grounds
(see, for example, reference [56]). I hope it's obvious,
however, that such criticisms are invalid, betraying
as they do a sad lack of understanding of the relational model.

- Applying the 20:20 hindsight principle once again, I
note that, despite its title, the 1970 paper nowhere
gives a succinct definition of the term *relational
model!*—nor indeed of the term *data model,* although

it was unquestionably the paper that introduced this latter concept too. On the contrary, it at least implies that the relational model consists of the structural aspects only (in other words, the manipulative and integrity aspects are excluded). In this connection, it's relevant to point out that the discussion of the relational operators in particular is included in the part of the paper called "Redundancy and Consistency," *not* in the part called "Relational Model and Normal Form."

Furthermore, the paper also talks about "*a* relational model . . . *for a data bank*" (my italics), thus unfortunately suggesting that the term "relational model" refers to an abstract view of the data *in a specific database,* instead of to an abstract view of data in general.

Both of the foregoing misconceptions are still regrettably all too common in the database literature; the first in particular—the idea that "the relational model is just structure," sometimes expressed in the form "the relational model is just flat files"—represents a *major* misconception, of course.

- Finally, a historical footnote: I was intrigued recently to come across a paper dating from *1966* (!) with the title "A Relational Model for Information Retrieval and the Processing of Linguistic Data" [3]. However, that paper is concerned not with database issues but with problems of natural language processing, and the "relational model" of the title is essentially a formalism for representing certain English sentences; for example, the sentence "John loves Mary" might be represented by the expression "*j* L *m*" (the relations of the paper are all binary). The ideas do have certain points in common with Codd's relational model (naturally, since they're based on the same logical foundation); however, I think it's fair to say that Codd still deserves the credit for being the sole inventor of the relational model of data, as we've come to understand that term in the database world.

Chapter 4

Codd's Relational Algebra

More on the foundations of the relational model

In 1972 Codd published another famous paper, "Relational Completeness of Data Base Sublanguages" [15]. Note that now he's talking about "data bases" instead of "data banks"!—but he hasn't yet quite made it all the way to *database* as one word (that didn't happen until 1979). Anyway, in this paper, Codd gives formal definitions for both a relational algebra and a relational calculus; he also defines the notion of relational completeness, gives an algorithm for transforming an arbitrary expression of the calculus into an equivalent expression of the algebra (thereby proving that the relational algebra is relationally complete), and argues in favor of the calculus over the algebra as a basis for a practical database language— quite a lot of territory to cover for such a comparatively short paper (only 36 double spaced pages, plus an abstract).

OVERVIEW OF THE PAPER

This paper—which I'll refer to from now on, for brevity, as *the completeness paper*—is perhaps the most formal of all Codd's relational publications. Certainly it's the most difficult for the average reader. It is, however, *fundamental,* in the sense that it rounds out the material of the first two papers [7,9] to complete the definition of what we now think of as the original relational model.

With regard to that "rounding out," incidentally, it's interesting to note that, like its predecessors [7,9], the completeness paper actually continues to talk as if the relational model consisted of structural aspects only: "In previous papers . . . we proposed a relational model of data . . . [Now] we define a collection of operations on relations . . ." (in other words, those operations are apparently not to be seen as part of the relational model *per se* but are an add-on). Nowadays, of course, we definitely do regard the operations as an integral part of the model, and what the completeness paper does is propose alternative but equivalent formalisms as a basis for that part.

Aside: I note in passing that the idea that operations *are* part of the model is very much in keeping with the modern perception that the *data type* concept includes the associated notion of operators that can legally be applied to instances of the type in question. Indeed, without the operators, the data is useless!—you can't do anything with it. That said, however, let me add that I definitely *don't* want my remarks here to be construed as meaning I think a relation is the same thing as a type. It isn't. It does *have* a type, but relations as such *are not* types. We might draw an analogy here with arrays; like a relation, an array *has* a type, but *is not* a type. (Actually "array" and "relation" are both examples of what are sometimes called *type generators*—see, e.g., reference [52]—but that's another topic I don't want to get into too much detail on here.) *End of aside.*

Let's take a high-level look at what the completeness paper achieves. To quote the abstract: "In the near future, we can expect a great variety of [proposals for database languages]. This paper [provides] a theoretical basis which may be used to determine how complete a selection capability is provided in [such a language]." That theoretical basis is the "relational completeness" of the paper's title; a language is said to be *relationally complete* if it's as powerful as the relational calculus (speaking a trifle loosely). Later in the paper, Codd asserts categorically that *every* general-purpose database language should be at least this powerful; in particular, he observes that, given such a language, queries can be formulated without the use of "programming loops or any other form of branched execution—an important consideration when interrogating a data base from a terminal" (and important too for access from within application programs, as we all now know).

By the way, the reason for saying merely that languages should be "at least" relationally complete is that (as Codd acknowledges) such completeness is only a *basic* measure of a language's power. Practical languages need other capabilities as well, as we'll see in Chapter 6.

Here then is the broad structure of the paper. There are five principal sections:

1. Introduction
2. A Relational Algebra
3. Relational Calculus
4. Reduction
5. Calculus *vs.* Algebra

Following the introduction, the paper gives a formal definition of a relational algebra—often now called, specifically, *Codd's* relational algebra, in order to distinguish it from other algebras that have been defined at various times—and a relational calculus. It then defines relational completeness in terms of the relational calculus. Next, it presents an algorithm ("Codd's reduction algorithm") for transforming an arbitrary expression of the calculus into an equivalent algebraic expression, thereby proving that the algebra is at least as powerful as the calculus and therefore relationally complete. Finally, it offers some opinions regarding the relative merits of the two formalisms (algebra and calculus) as a basis for the design of a practical database language.

The remainder of the present chapter is devoted to Codd's relational algebra *per se.*

RELATIONAL ALGEBRA OPERATIONS

According to *Chambers Twentieth Century Dictionary,* an *algebra* is "any of a number of systems using symbols and involving reasoning about relationships and operations." More specifically, an algebra consists of a set of *objects* and a set of *operators* that together satisfy certain *axioms* or *laws* (such as closure, commutativity, associativity, and so on). The word "algebra" itself ultimately derives from Arabic *al-jebr,* meaning a *resetting* (of something broken) or a *combination.*

In relational algebra specifically, of course, the objects are relations; the operations are things like restriction, projection, join, and so forth; and there are several axioms or laws, including in particular the crucially important one—oddly enough not mentioned explicitly, but most certainly implied, in the completeness paper—of *closure:* **The result of any relational operation is always another relation.** As I've explained elsewhere (see, e.g., references [32] and [49]), closure has the important consequence that we can write *nested relational expressions.*

A few more preliminary remarks:

- The algebraic operations are all *read-only* (that is, they all serve merely to derive some relation from other relations, loosely speaking). Note, therefore, that they operate very specifically on relation *values.* From the point of view of relational algebra, there's no need for, and no such thing as, a relation *variable.* Of course, a real database language will presumably support update operations as well (at the very least a relational *assignment* operation), and will therefore require relation variables too, but such matters are not part of the relational algebra *per se.*

- For "notational and expository convenience," Codd's paper assumes that "domains of relations"—he really means attributes or columns—are identified by ordinal position, not by name (though he does recognize that names are better in practice). As a result, he doesn't get into the question of *column names of results,* which is actually an important aspect of closure, and he doesn't discuss the need for a *column rename* operator. See reference [49] for a detailed discussion of these issues. In what follows, I'll use column names rather than numbers.

- The paper—very unfortunately, in my opinion!—says that "for data base purposes, we are concerned with data consisting of integers and character strings." This remark might possibly be the source of the misconception, widespread to this very day, that relational systems are capable of dealing only with very simple data such as integers and strings. (The paper does also say that "other types of primitive elements may be included," but *this* remark merely brings us back to the thorny question of what "primitive," or "atomic," data might be [42].) The strange thing is that the paper nowhere relies on the "simple data" assumption, at least not in any significant way.

Anyway, Codd goes on to define the following algebraic operations:

- Cartesian product
- Union, intersection, and difference
- θ-restriction
- Projection
- θ-join and natural join
- Division
- Factoring

I don't propose to give definitions of all of these operations here, since such definitions can be found in many other places (see reference [49], for example); however, I will just note a few differences between Codd's definitions and those usually adopted today, and comment on certain related matters of interest.

Cartesian product:　Strictly speaking, the Cartesian product of two relations is a set of *pairs* of the form (a,b), where a is a tuple from the first operand relation and b is a tuple from the second. (Incidentally, the completeness paper seems to be the first in which Codd uses "tuple" as an abbreviation for n-tuple.) Because of the closure objective, however, we want the result to be a relation specifically. Codd therefore defines an *expanded* version of Cartesian product, which produces a set of tuples instead of a set of pairs. More precisely, where the regular Cartesian product would have produced the pair (a,b), the expanded version produces a tuple consisting of all components of a together with all components of b. The expanded product operation—unlike the regular one—is both commutative and associative, meaning we can talk unambiguously of the product of n relations for any n. (We can even allow n to be one or zero, though Codd doesn't explicitly discuss these possibilities.)

Union, intersection, difference:　This paper was the first to mention the specifically relational versions of these operations, in which the operands are required to be "union-compatible" (so that again the result is always another relation). Union and intersection (but not difference) are both commutative and associative.

θ-**restriction:**   "θ" here stands for any of the usual comparison operations (=, <, and so on). If *A* and *B* are attributes of relation *R,* the θ-restriction of *R* on *A* and *B* (in that order) is defined to be a relation with the same attributes as *R* and containing just those tuples of *R* for which the condition "*A* θ *B*" is *true.* Note that this definition is different from the one given in reference [9]. Note too that attributes are allowed to be "compound"—for example, the simple attributes STREET, CITY, STATE, and ZIP might together be regarded as a compound attribute ADDR—though Codd doesn't address the question of what a comparison such as "*A* < *B*" might mean if *A* and *B* are compound in this sense.

Projection: This operation is basically as understood today. Codd makes the important observation that projection provides an algebraic counterpart to the *existential quantifier* of relational calculus. *Note:* The paper adopts the convention that the projection of a relation *R* over no attributes at all is simply *R.* This convention is unfortunate, however, because projecting over no attributes at all should actually yield a *nullary relation*—specifically, either TABLE_DEE or TABLE_DUM [33].

θ-**join and natural join:**   These operations are also basically as understood today. But it's interesting to note that Codd defines natural join—almost as an afterthought, it would seem—in terms of θ-join (more precisely, as a projection of an equijoin). Today we would tend to regard natural join as being the more fundamental operation (so much so that the unqualified term "join" is usually taken to mean the natural join specifically). Indeed, you might have noticed that "θ-joins" as such weren't even mentioned in Codd's first two papers either [7,9]. Further, Codd does note that θ-join can be defined in terms of θ-restriction, so it's not a primitive operation. (Actually, the opposite is true as well—that is, θ-restriction can be defined in terms of θ-join. Which collection of operations we choose to regard as primitive is thus somewhat arbitrary; it depends on where we stand. One commonly accepted primitive collection is restriction, projection, product, union, and difference.) *Note:* Like the union, intersection, and (expanded) product operations, natural join is both commutative and associative.

Division: The completeness paper was the first to mention this operation; in fact, it's clear that Codd introduced it here specifically to serve as "an algebraic counterpart to the universal quantifier" in his reduction algorithm. He does note that it isn't primitive—it can be defined in terms of the operations already described. (As a matter of fact, the definition is not quite the same as the one we use today, but the differences are minor. Perhaps more to the point, I should mention that it's possible to define a version of the operation that—unlike the one defined in the paper—allows any relation to be divided by any relation, as I've explained elsewhere [36].)

By the way, have you ever wondered why the operation is called "division"? The following identity shows why:

```
( R TIMES S ) DIVIDEBY S  ≡  R
```

(I'm assuming here that relation S is nonempty.) In other words, division is a kind of inverse of Cartesian product.

Note: I should point out that, in a sense, division *isn't* quite the counterpart to the universal quantifier that it was meant to be; it suffers from problems having to do with empty sets and related matters, as I've explained in reference [36]. In fact, Codd himself gives an example that illustrates the problem: Given a relation SP { S#, P#, . . . } showing which suppliers supply which parts, he claims that the expression

```
SP { S#, P# } DIVIDEBY SP { P# }
```

will give supplier numbers for suppliers who supply all parts. However, if there happen to be no parts at all (and hence no shipments), this expression gives the wrong answer (it gives no supplier numbers at all, whereas it should give them all).

In any case, I now think that *relational comparisons* provide a better basis for dealing with the kinds of problems that division was intended to solve [37]—but, of course, the relational model as originally defined by Codd didn't include such comparisons at all.

Factoring: This operation (which today is more usually called *nesting*) converts a normalized relation to unnormalized form. Given the normalized relation EMP, for example, with attributes EMP# and DEPT#, the operation could be used to produce an unnormalized relation with attributes DEPT# and SET_OF_EMPS, in which each tuple contains a department number and a set of all corresponding employee numbers. *Note:* This operation isn't used at all in the body of the paper; its definition is relegated to an appendix, and Codd suggests that it might be useful "for presentation purposes" merely. I should say too that our understanding of the true nature of normalization has improved since 1971; in fact, we now regard *all* relations, even ones involving attributes whose values are relations, as normalized. "Unnormalized relation" is thus something of a contradiction in terms. However, it is at least true (from a database design point of view) that relations involving relation-valued attributes are often contraindicated.

CONCLUDING REMARKS

This brings me to the end of my discussion of Codd's relational algebra *per se*. In the next chapter, I'll continue this examination of the completeness paper by taking a look at Codd's relational calculus and related matters.

Chapter 5

Codd's Relational Calculus

*The foundations of the relational
model, continued*

In this chapter, I want to complete my retrospective review (begun in the previous chapter) of Codd's completeness paper [15], looking at the relational calculus portions in particular. Just to remind you, the paper contains formal definitions of both a relational algebra and a relational calculus; it also defines the concept of relational completeness, gives an algorithm for transforming an arbitrary calculus expression into an equivalent algebraic one, and offers some arguments in favor of the calculus over the algebra as a basis for a practical database language. Note that since they are equivalent, either the calculus or the algebra can be regarded as the basis for the manipulative part of the relational model.

RELATIONAL CALCULUS:
AN OVERVIEW

Relational calculus is an applied form of a fundamental branch of logic called *predicate* calculus. In general, the term "calculus" signifies merely a *system of computation* (the Latin word *calculus* means a pebble, perhaps used in counting or some other form of reckoning). Thus, relational calculus can be thought of as a system for computing with relations. *Note:* The relational calculus we'll be concerned with here is sometimes called, specifically, *Codd's* relational calculus, in order to distinguish it from others that have been defined at various times since.

Essentially, relational calculus provides a notation for writing down the definition of some relation in terms of others (usually). Such definitions—which can clearly serve among other things as the basis for the formulation of queries—typically involve one or more *range variables*. A range variable (actually called a *tuple* variable in the completeness paper) is a variable that "ranges over" some relation; that is, it's a variable whose only permitted values are tuples of the relation in question. Thus, if range variable r ranges over relation R, then, at any given time, the expression r denotes some tuple of R. Consider the language QUEL [55], for example, which is a calculus-based language. Given the usual suppliers and parts database, the query "Get supplier numbers and cities for suppliers with status greater than 10" might be expressed in QUEL as follows:

```
RANGE OF SX IS S
RETRIEVE ( SX.S#, SX.CITY ) WHERE SX.STATUS > 10
```

The range variable here is SX, and it ranges over relation S (the RANGE statement is a *declaration* for that variable). The RETRIEVE statement might be paraphrased: "For each possible value of the variable SX, retrieve the S# and CITY components of that value, if and only if the STATUS component has a value greater than 10."

Note: You might think it a little perverse of me to use QUEL as the basis for examples, given that Codd himself defined a calculus-based language called ALPHA in reference [11], but I do have my reasons—the main one being that I want to discuss ALPHA in detail in the next chapter.

RELATIONAL CALCULUS EXPRESSIONS

Reference [15] presents the relational calculus bottom up. However, I think it's a little easier to understand if it's presented top down, so that's what I'll do here. (I do want to be a little more complete in my presentation of the calculus than I was in my presentation of the algebra in the previous chapter, because the calculus does tend to be less well understood. Nevertheless, I will as usual omit many details and simplify others, and I'll use my own syntax, mostly, instead of that of reference [15].)

Alpha expressions: A calculus query is represented by an *alpha expression,* which takes the form

```
( target-commalist ) WHERE qualification
```

where:

- The *target-commalist* is a list of expressions of the form $r.A$, separated by commas. Here r is the name of a range variable and A is the name of an attribute of the relation over which r ranges; the expression $r.A$ denotes the A component of the tuple currently denoted by r. *Note:* As in his discussion of the algebra (see Chapter 4), Codd actually uses ordinal positions, not names, to refer to attributes (thus using the expression $r[i]$ to refer to the "ith component" of the tuple currently denoted by r). I prefer to use names.

- The overall alpha expression evaluates to a certain relation, as follows. Let the (distinct) range variables appearing in the target-commalist be $r1, r2, \ldots, rn$. Let the corresponding relations be $R1, R2, \ldots, Rn$, respectively. Let X be the Cartesian product of $R1$, $R2, \ldots, Rn$. Let Y be a relation derived from X by deleting those tuples that fail to satisfy the *qualification* (I'll explain that "qualification" in detail in a moment; here let me just note that omitting it is equivalent to specifying simply *true*). Let Z be a projection of Y, defined in the obvious way in accordance with the attributes mentioned in the target-commalist. Then Z is the relation denoted by the overall expression.

Refer back to the QUEL example shown earlier for a simple example of an alpha expression (or at least the QUEL version of such an expression). Note that the RETRIEVE keyword in that QUEL example is essentially just noise (as is SELECT in SQL, come to that).

Qualifications: A qualification is a *well-formed formula* (WFF, variously pronounced "weff," "wiff," or "woof"), defined in accordance with the following simple grammar:

```
wff  ::=   TRUE
         | FALSE
         | comparison
         | NOT wff
         | ( wff AND wff )
         | ( wff OR wff )
         | EXISTS r ( wff )
         | FORALL r ( wff )
```

TRUE and FALSE here are literals, denoting the values *true* and *false,* respectively, and *comparison* is an expression of the form "$r.A \; \theta \; s.B$" (where r and s are range variables, A and B are attributes, and—as in Chapter 4—"θ" stands for any of the usual comparison operators). Thus, the semantics of WFFs in general should be pretty obvious (except perhaps for those involving EXISTS or FORALL—I'll get to those in a moment).

Note: Reference [15] additionally requires the qualification to include a set of expressions defining the ranges of the range variables that appear "free" in the WFF (see below for an explanation of free variables). By contrast, I choose to assume for simplicity that those definitions have been factored out into separate RANGE declarations, as in QUEL. Observe that:

- All range variables in the target-commalist must be free; by contrast, range variables in the qualification can be either free or bound.

- All range variables that appear free in the qualification must also appear (necessarily free) in the target-commalist.

I should mention too that reference [15] also allows range variables to range over unions, intersections, and differences of the given relations, as well as over the given relations as such. I omit the details here. Of course, all relations involved in such a union or intersection or difference must be "union-compatible" (see Chapter 4).

Quantifiers and free *vs.* bound variables: Each appearance of a range variable within a given expression is either *free* or *bound*. Within a WFF, the only possible ways a range variable *r* can appear are (a) within a comparison, in an attribute reference of the form *r.a;* (b) immediately following one of the quantifiers EXISTS and FORALL. Here then are the rules governing whether a given appearance of a given range variable ("appearance" for short) in a given WFF is free or bound:

- Within the comparison "*r.A* θ *s.B,*" all appearances are free.
- Appearances in NOT *w* are free or bound according as they are free or bound in *w*. Appearances in (*w1* AND *w2*) and (*w1* OR *w2*) are free or bound according as they are free or bound in *w1* or *w2* (whichever is applicable).
- Appearances of *r* that are free in *w* are bound in EXISTS *r* (*w*) and FORALL *r* (*w*). Other appearances in *w* are free or bound in these WFFs according as they are free or bound in *w*.

Now I can explain the quantifiers. If *w* is a WFF in which *r* is free, then EXISTS *r* (*w*) and FORALL *r* (*w*) are both legal WFFs (and r is bound in both of them). The first means: There exists at least one value of r such that w evaluates to *true*. The second means: For all values of r, w evaluates to *true*.

Note: As I've explained elsewhere [49], bound variables act as a kind of *dummy*. For example, suppose relation R has just one attribute, A, defined on the domain of integers, and let $r1$ and $r2$ be range variables that range over R. Consider the WFF EXISTS $r1$ ($r1.A > 3$). This WFF simply states that there exists some tuple in R in which the A-value is greater than three. Note, therefore, that the meaning of the WFF would be completely unchanged if all appearances of $r1$ were replaced by appearances of $r2$; that is, the WFF EXISTS $r2$ ($r2.A > 3$) is semantically identical to the previous one.

Now consider the WFF EXISTS $r1$ ($r1.A > 3$) AND $r1.A < 0$. Here there are three appearances of $r1$, and they refer to *two different variables*. The first two appearances are bound, and could be replaced by $r2$ without changing the overall meaning. The third appearance is free, and *cannot* be replaced with impunity. Of the two WFFs below, therefore, the first is equivalent to the one just mentioned but the second isn't:

- EXISTS $r2$ ($r2.A > 3$) AND $r1.A < 0$
- EXISTS $r2$ ($r2.A > 3$) AND $r2.A < 0$

Note too that the truth value of the original WFF cannot be determined without knowing the value of the free variable $r1$. By contrast, a WFF in which all variables are bound is *true* or *false,* unequivocally.

EXAMPLES

In this section, I'll give a few examples to illustrate the ideas introduced in the previous section. The examples are all based on the usual suppliers and parts database. I'll use RANGE statements to declare the necessary range variables—in fact, I'll assume throughout that the following declarations are in effect:

```
RANGE OF SX IS S
RANGE OF SY IS S
RANGE OF SPX IS SP
RANGE OF PX IS P
```

- Get supplier numbers and names for suppliers in Paris with status less than 20.

```
( SX.S#, SX.SNAME ) WHERE ( SX.CITY = "Paris"
                      AND   SX.STATUS < 20 )
```

All appearances of SX here are free.

- Get all supplier-number/part-number pairs such that the supplier and part are located in the same city.

```
( SX.S#, PX.P# ) WHERE SX.CITY = PX.CITY
```

Again, all range variable appearances are free.

- Get all pairs of supplier numbers such that the two suppliers are located in the same city.

```
( SX.S# AS FIRSTS#, SY.S# AS SECONDS# )
  WHERE SX.CITY = SY.CITY
```

Once again all range variable appearances are free. Note the use of the specifications "AS FIRSTS#" and "AS SECONDS#" here to introduce names for attributes of the result. The calculus as defined in reference

[15] includes no such feature, since it deals with attribute numbers instead of attribute names.

- Get supplier names for suppliers who supply part P2.

```
( SX.SNAME ) WHERE EXISTS SPX
             ( ( SPX.S# = SX.S# AND SPX.P# = "P2" )
```

Here SX is free throughout and SPX is bound throughout.

- Get supplier names for suppliers who supply at least one red part.

```
( SX.SNAME ) WHERE EXISTS SPX
             ( ( SPX.S# = SX.S# AND
                 EXISTS PX ( ( PX.P# = SPX.P# AND
                               PX.COLOR = "Red" ) ) )
```

This example illustrates a clear need for rules allowing unnecessary parentheses to be dropped!

- Get supplier names for suppliers who supply all parts.

```
( SX.SNAME ) WHERE FORALL PX
             ( EXISTS SPX ( ( SPX.S# = SX.S# AND
                             SPX.P# = PX.P# ) ) )
```

- Get supplier names for suppliers who do not supply part P2.

```
( SX.SNAME ) WHERE NOT EXISTS SPX
             ( ( SPX.S# = SX.S# AND SPX.P# = "P2" ) )
```

CODD'S REDUCTION ALGORITHM

After presenting the relational calculus, reference [15] goes on to describe an algorithm ("Codd's reduction algorithm") by which an arbitrary expression of the calculus can be reduced to a semantically equivalent expression of the algebra. I don't intend to explain the algorithm in detail here, but I do want to discuss a couple of implications of the fact that the algorithm exists.

1. *The algebra can serve as a vehicle for implementing the calculus.* That is, given a calculus-based language like QUEL, one approach to implementing that language would be to take the query as submitted by the user—which is basically just a calculus expression—and apply the reduction algorithm to it, thereby obtaining an equivalent algebraic expression. That algebraic expression will consist of a set of algebraic operations, which are by definition inherently implementable. *Note:* In fact, a pioneering paper on optimization [57] is based on exactly this approach to implementation; it implements the given calculus expression by executing an appropriate sequence of algebraic operations, applying a variety of optimizations to those operations as it does so.

2. A language *L* is said to be *relationally complete* if it's at least as powerful as the relational calculus—that is, if any relation definable by some expression of the relational calculus is also definable by some expression of *L*. As we saw in Chapter 4, Codd suggests (and I agree) that every general-purpose database language ought to be at least this powerful.

   Now, it follows immediately from the existence of the reduction algorithm that Codd's relational algebra is relationally complete. To show that some language is relationally complete, therefore, it's sufficient (and usually easier) to show that it's as powerful as the algebra, rather than the calculus. For example, to show that SQL is relationally complete (which it is), we have to demonstrate (a) that there exist SQL expressions for each of the five primitive operations restrict, project, product, union, and difference, and then (b) that the operands to those SQL expressions can be arbitrary SQL expressions in turn (meaning that the operations can be nested and combined in arbitrary ways). Such a demonstration can be found in reference [49].

CALCULUS *VS.* ALGEBRA

Codd's reduction algorithm shows that the algebra is at least as powerful as the calculus. As you might expect, it's also possible to show the converse as well: namely, that the calculus is at least as powerful as the algebra—see, for example, reference [60]. It follows that the two are equivalent. *Note:* As a matter of fact, the calculus as defined in reference [15] is *not* quite as powerful as the algebra, because it lacks the ability to express a union of two projections—for example, S {CITY} UNION P {CITY}. This slight defect is easily remedied, of course. Also, I should mention in passing that Codd's reduction algorithm actually had a tiny error in it [31], again easily fixed.

By the way, you will sometimes hear people characterize the difference between the algebra and the calculus as being analogous to that between procedural and nonprocedural languages. In other words, the algebra is *prescriptive* (procedural), while the calculus is *descriptive* (nonprocedural). While this characterization might be helpful from an intuitive point of view, I hope you understand that it isn't really accurate, given the complete interchangeability of the two formalisms. In other words, the difference is largely one of style, not of true substance.

Be that as it may, Codd concludes his paper with some brief arguments in favor of using the calculus over the algebra as a basis for a practical database language. His arguments are as follows (paraphrasing somewhat):

1. *Extendability:* Relational completeness is only a *basic* measure of expressive power (as the paper puts it, "in a practical environment it would need to be augmented by a counting and summing capability, together with the capability of invoking [many other] library functions"). Extending the calculus to support invocations of such functions seems straightforward:

   a. They could be used within a target-commalist to transform the data retrieved in some way;

   b. They could be used to generate a comparand within a comparison within a qualification;

   c. If they return a truth value, they could be used in place of a comparison within a qualification.

   Codd claims that, by contrast, extending the algebra seems much less straightforward and would "give rise to circumlocutions." I'm not sure I agree with this position, however; grafting the operators EXTEND and SUMMARIZE on to the original relational algebra (which is more or less what's needed to do the job) seems fairly straightforward to me [49].

2. *Ease of capturing the user's intent* (important for optimization, authorization, and so forth): Because it permits the user to request data by its properties instead of by means of manipulative operations, the calculus is a better basis than the algebra for this purpose. (Again I'm not sure I agree—given that any request that can be stated as a single calculus expression can equally well be stated as a single algebraic expression.)

3. *Closeness to natural language:* Codd recognizes that most users should not have to deal directly with either the algebra or the calculus as such. But the idea of requesting data by its properties is more natural than that of having to devise an appropriate set of manipulative operations. Thus the calculus should prove more suitable as a target for some more user-friendly higher-level language. (Once again, I don't really agree, for essentially the same reason as under 2. above. But I do want to point out that because they are more systematically defined, the calculus and the algebra are *both* much more suitable than SQL as such a target! In this connection, it's worth noting that many SQL systems effectively convert SQL internally into something rather close to the algebra for implementation purposes.)

Chapter 6

Data Sublanguage ALPHA

Part 1 of 2

A look at Codd's own proposal
for a relational language

In the previous chapter, I mentioned the fact that Codd himself originally proposed a database language—"Data Sublanguage ALPHA"—based on the relational calculus. He described that language (albeit only informally) as early as 1970 [8] and again, more fully, in 1971 [11]; in fact, ALPHA was probably the very first relational language to be described by anyone, anywhere. Although ALPHA itself was never implemented, it was very influential on the design of subsequent languages that definitely were, including in particular QUEL and—to a lesser extent—SQL; moreover, it also included some useful ideas (such as quota queries) that are still to this day not widely supported. In this chapter and the next, I want to take a look at some of the salient features of ALPHA. I'll use reference [11] as my primary source (referring to it in what follows as "the ALPHA paper" or sometimes just "Codd's paper"); I'll mention reference [8] specifically only in connection with certain interesting ideas that didn't make it into reference [11].

Before I get into the specifics of ALPHA *per se,* let me just mention that the ALPHA paper also includes a short list of "principal motivations of the relational model." I'll come back to this aspect of the paper in a later chapter.

WORKSPACES

Because it's intended as a *sub*language specifically, ALPHA requires some mechanism for exchanging data with the host language in which it happens to be embedded. *Workspaces* serve this purpose. The basic idea is that data retrieved from the database via an ALPHA operation is placed in a specified workspace, where it can be accessed by means of the host language; in a similar manner, data generated by the host language can be placed in such a workspace and then transferred to the database via another ALPHA operation. From ALPHA's point of view, therefore, a workspace contains a relation (or sometimes a tuple); from the host's point of view, by contrast, it contains an *array representation* of such a relation or tuple (where the "array" in question includes a special row of column names).

ALPHA's reliance on workspaces effectively means that it embraces the concept of a *two-level store,* meaning that the user sees a sharp distinction between data in main memory and data in the database. This distinction—which is, of course, a consequence of the fact that ALPHA is a *sub*language specifically—has been perpetuated in many other languages, including in particular SQL. It has also been the subject of some criticism (see, e.g., reference [26]). In *The Third Manifesto,* by contrast [25,52], Hugh Darwen and I suggest that users should be able to operate in terms of a *one*-level store; data transfers between memory levels are an implementation detail merely and ought preferably to be hidden from the user.

AN OVERVIEW OF ALPHA

Codd states explicitly that he "does not attach any special importance to the syntax of ALPHA"; however, he does have to use *some* syntax in describing the language, and I'll use that same syntax here, more or less. I'll show keywords of that syntax in **bold** in order to set them off from surrounding text.

The following feature summary gives some idea of the scope of the ALPHA language:

- Introducing and removing domain names: **DOMAIN, DROP**
- Declaring and destroying relations: **RELATION, DROP**
- Declaring range ("tuple") variables: **RANGE**
- Retrieval: **GET**
- Insertion: **PUT**
- Modification: **HOLD, UPDATE, RELEASE**
- Deletion: **DELETE**
- "Piped mode": **OPEN, CLOSE**

Let's take a closer look at each of these features in turn.

DATA DEFINITION OPERATIONS

I'll start with domains. The only domains mentioned in the ALPHA paper are "simple" ones—that is, ones represented in terms of "simple" data types like **CHAR(5)**, **NUM(4,0)**, and so on. In other words, domains seem to be little more than what the SQL standard calls "DISTINCT types" [51], instead of being full abstract data types— ADTs—in all their glory. (On the other hand, there's nothing in the paper to suggest they *can't* be full ADTs!) Anyway, here's an example of defining (and subsequently destroying) an ALPHA domain:

```
DOMAIN CITY CHAR(15)

DROP CITY
```

One good thing about the paper is that—unlike some of those that preceded it—it does make a clear distinction between domains and attributes. In fact, it adopts a convention that attribute names take the specific form

```
[role-name_]domain-name
```

where the optional *role-name* is a qualifier that's needed only if the same domain is used more than once in the same relation. "One important advantage of [this scheme is that it permits] systematic handling of *all-occurrence transformations* . . . An example . . . is a sweeping change of all part numbers wherever they occur. . . ." Here Codd seems to be at least partly overlooking the role the *catalog* could play in such a transformation—an odd omission, considering that he does mention the catalog explicitly later in the paper. (Indeed, one of the many important firsts that can be chalked up to the ALPHA paper

is the suggestion that the catalog itself should be structured in the same way as the rest of the data—i.e., as relations.) In other words, I'm not convinced that the
attribute naming convention is a very good one. And indeed it clearly isn't, when we take into account the question of attribute names for *derived* relations.

Turning now to relations—more precisely, to what
Codd calls "time-varying" relations—note first that the
bulk of the paper makes a tacit assumption that all such
relations are *base* relations specifically; such matters as
view definition, and especially view updating, receive essentially no attention (though the earlier draft [8] does
include a brief discussion of a view-related phenomenon
it calls "domain migration," which I'll discuss in the next
chapter). The definition of such a relation specifies the *relation name,* the *attribute* names (and hence, implicitly,
the corresponding domains), and the *primary key.* Here's
an example of such a definition (together with a corresponding DROP):

```
RELATION S ( S#, SNAME_NAME, STATUS, CITY ) KEY S#
DROP S
```

Note: For simplicity, I'll abbreviate SNAME_NAME
to just SNAME from this point forward (as indeed I already did in Chapter 5).

DATA MANIPULATION OPERATIONS

Retrieval: Here's an ALPHA retrieval example ("get supplier names and cities for suppliers who supply all parts"):

```
RANGE S  SX
RANGE SP SPX
RANGE P  PX
GET W1 ( SX.SNAME, SX.CITY ) :
     ALL PX SOME SPX ( SPX.S# = SX.S# AND SPX.P# = PX.P# )
```

Here W1 is the name of the applicable workspace, the colon (":") can be read as "where" or "such that," and **ALL** and **SOME** denote the universal and the existential quantifier, respectively. *Note:* Actually, reference [11] uses the standard logic symbols for **ALL** and **SOME** (also for the connectives **AND, OR,** and so on); reference [8], by contrast, uses the keywords, which I prefer. Reference [11] also allows the quantifiers to be moved up into the **RANGE** declarations, as here:

```
RANGE S  SX
RANGE SP SPX SOME
RANGE P  PX  ALL

GET W1 ( SX.SNAME, SX.CITY ) : SPX.S# = SX.S# AND
                               SPX.P# = PX.P#
```

Note: Reference [11] never mentions the possibility of a range variable ranging over, for example, the union of two base relations, or indeed over anything more complex than a single base relation (though I did discuss this possibility in the previous chapter). Also, the earlier paper [8] uses the keyword **DUMMY** in place of **RANGE,** on the grounds that (as I also discussed in the previous chapter) a range variable can be thought of as a kind of "dummy" variable.

GET operations also permit:

- References to relations in workspaces just as if they were in the database. Such references use the workspace name for qualification purposes just as if it were a relation name.

- Specification of a tuple ordering for the result (analogous to SQL's ORDER BY), using the keywords **UP** and **DOWN**.

- Specification of a *quota* to limit the number of tuples retrieved. The paper does not, however, address the question of what should happen if the result relation is thereby not uniquely determined [43].

- The use of certain truth-valued functions (**TOP** and **BOTTOM**) in the qualification. **TOP** and **BOTTOM** are ALPHA's analogs of the functions IS_NTH_LARGEST and IS_NTH_SMALLEST described in reference [43].

- The use of certain *aggregate functions* (**COUNT, TOTAL, MAX, MIN, AVERAGE**) in the target-commalist (the term "aggregate functions" isn't used, however). *Note:* The original version of the paper overlooked the fact that, at least for **TOTAL** and **AVERAGE,** the argument is a *bag,* not a set (duplicates shouldn't be eliminated before the aggregation is performed). Codd later acknowledged this error [14].

As an aside, I remark that ALPHA does *not* directly permit aggregate functions to appear in the qualification; instead, it makes use of a shorthand version called *image* functions (which can also be used in the target-commalist). I'll skip the details here, since frankly I don't think image functions were one of ALPHA's better ideas. Indeed, they might well have been the source of the strange syntax used in both QUEL and SQL for aggregate function invocations, and hence for the complexities caused in both languages by that unorthodox syntax. (The complexities in question are caused by the fact that function arguments are determined, in part, *by reference to context* [27,28], instead of—as would have been more orthodox—being fully determined by whatever's specified within the parentheses immediately following the function name.)

ALPHA also permits retrieval to be performed a tuple at a time via *piped mode* (analogous to SQL's FETCH via a cursor). For example (assuming the same **RANGE** declarations as before):

```
OPEN GET W1 ( SX.SNAME, SX.CITY ) :
             SPX.S# = SX.S# AND SPX.P# = PX.P# UP SX.CITY
...
GET W1
/* now process current tuple via host language */
...
CLOSE W1
```

Each execution of **GET** W1 here retrieves the next tuple from the result of the query in the **OPEN** (note the **UP** ordering specification in that **OPEN**). *Note:* Of course, piped mode opens up the possibility of *subverting the system,* because it can be used to perform what is essentially "manual navigation" (instead of the *automatic* navigation normally preferred in a relational system [17]). But of course piped mode or something like it is essential if the language is indeed meant to be a *sub*language specifically, as ALPHA is.

Insertion: The PUT operation transfers a set of tuples from a specified workspace to a specified relation. For example:

```
PUT W2 SP
```

("insert the tuples in workspace W2 into relation SP"). An ordering can be specified too, to inform the system that the tuples to be inserted are ordered in a certain way in the workspace. (Actually I feel a little uncomfortable with this particular notion; it seems to me to mix logical and physical ideas too much.)

"Piped insertion" is also possible:

```
OPEN PUT W2 S
...
/* construct current tuple via host language */
PUT W2
...
CLOSE W2
```

Modification: Here's a data modification example ("move all Paris suppliers to Rome"):

```
HOLD W3 ( SX.S#, SX.CITY ) : SX.CITY = 'Paris'
/* set CITY to 'Rome' in every workspace tuple */
/* via host language                          */
UPDATE W3
```

ALPHA requires tuples that are to be updated to be retrieved first, via **HOLD** (there's no analog of SQL's out-of-the-blue "searched UPDATE"). The **HOLD** target-commalist must involve exactly one range variable (SX in the example), meaning the **UPDATE** will be applied to just one (base) relation. (As Codd puts it, "[the single range variable restriction] avoids unwarranted complexity." Just so!) If the user decides not to perform the **UP-DATE** after all, the operation **RELEASE** W3 can be executed to release the held tuples.

Note: Although reference [11] doesn't say as much, the **HOLD** target-commalist must include all primary key attributes of the relation to be modified, so that the system can know which tuples are to be updated [14]. Primary key attributes themselves cannot be directly updated via a **HOLD . . . UPDATE** sequence, but deletions and insertions can be used to achieve an analogous effect.

Piped mode is also available for **HOLD . . . UPDATE/ RELEASE** (analogous to SQL's UPDATE CURRENT). Oddly, there's no analog of DELETE CURRENT. The omission is unimportant, however, because—as I've argued elsewhere [41]—modifying or deleting (or indeed inserting) a single tuple is a very bad idea anyway. Update operations should *always* be set-at-a-time.

You can probably tell that the modification portions of ALPHA aren't exactly its strongpoint; indeed, the foregoing discussions raise many questions which the paper simply doesn't address at all . . . Let's hurry on!

Deletion: DELETE operations are basically straightforward, apart from the criticisms already mentioned that apply to update operations in general. Here's an example:

```
DELETE SX : SX.S# = 'S1'
```

Chapter 7

Data Sublanguage ALPHA

Part 2 of 2

*Concluding our brief look at
Codd's ALPHA language*

In the previous chapter, I began my examination of Codd's *Data Sublanguage ALPHA,* taking a look at the basic data definition and data manipulation operations of that language. Now I want to conclude that examination; more specifically, I want to consider a number of miscellaneous issues that I had no room to cover in the previous chapter. As before, I'll use reference [11] as my primary source (referring to it as "the ALPHA paper" or sometimes just "Codd's paper"); I'll mention reference [8] specifically only in connection with material that didn't make it into reference [11] for some reason.

MISCELLANEOUS ISSUES

Implicit range variables: ALPHA supports the obvious shorthand of allowing relation names to be used in place of explicit range variable names so long as no ambiguity results. A relation name used in this way denotes an *implicit* range variable that ranges over the relation in question. Thus, the retrieval example from the previous chapter ("get supplier names and cities for suppliers who supply all parts") might have been expressed as follows:

```
GET W1 ( S.SNAME, S.CITY ) :
      ALL P SOME SP ( SP.S# = S.S# AND SP.P# = P.P# )
```

But it's important to understand that the name "S" here does *not* represent the suppliers relation S—it represents a *range variable* called S that ranges over the relation with that same name (and similarly for the names P and SP). Both QUEL and SQL adopted such a shorthand, of course.

Dual mode: In reference [11], Codd explicitly talks about what we now call the *dual-mode principle,* according to which any database operation that can be invoked interactively can also be invoked from within an application program: "[ALPHA] is intended to be a sublanguage . . . of the languages used by all terminal users . . . It is also intended to be a sublanguage of such host programming languages as PL/I, COBOL, and FORTRAN." Another first, I believe.

Catalog: As I mentioned in Chapter 6, the ALPHA paper shows clearly that Codd was aware of the significance of the catalog. In particular, it explicitly states that the catalog itself should be structured as relations: "The catalog . . . can itself be a part of the data base and would then consist of . . . relations." And later: "All of the information regarding a new relation—relation name, attribute and domain names, primary key specification, and so on—must be entered in those relations that catalog the data base relations" (slightly paraphrased). And: "The access authorization constraints must be set up in those relations which describe these constraints . . . A storage representation must be selected for the new relation (this may include a decision as to which attributes are to be indexed), and this descriptive information must be stored in appropriate relations."

Indirect references: ALPHA includes a *dereferencing* operator called PER, according to which (for example) the operation

```
GET W2 PER ( W1.X )
```

retrieves into workspace W2 the relation whose name is given in the X component of workspace W1. QUEL had a somewhat similar feature; SQL didn't, until the "dynamic SQL" feature was introduced.

Domain migration: Reference [8] includes some remarks on what it calls *domain migration* (*attribute* migration would be a better term). The basic idea is that some attribute might "migrate" from one base relation to another, loosely speaking, and we would like our queries and applications to continue to function correctly after such a migration. In other words, Codd is talking here about one aspect of what we would now call *logical data indepen-dence*. The general solution to this problem, of course, is to provide *views* that make the new relations look like the old ones as far as those queries and applications are con-cerned. And that solution is essentially what Codd pro-poses (though he doesn't use the term "view" as such). *Note:* Reference [11] touches on the foregoing ideas only very obliquely (it certainly doesn't get into any details).

Three-valued logic: The ALPHA paper—very unfor-tunately, in my opinion!—permits a retrieval operation to include the qualifier MAYBE_TOO, to indicate that tuples should be returned for which the qualification evaluates to *unknown* (the paper refers to this truth value as *maybe*), as well as those for which it evaluates to *true*. In other words, Codd was suggesting that the system should be based on three-valued logic and should support some kind of *null* (which he refers to as "the absent value"). He didn't elaborate on this idea at all in the paper, except for:

a. Giving a simple example of inserting tuples for which not all components are specified ("the system [inserts] the absent value [for those missing components]"), and

b. Remarking that "the ramifications [of such an ap-proach] are substantial."

I fear this latter observation is all too true. As you might already know, Codd and I disagree strongly on the merits of nulls and three-valued logic, and I'm sorry to see him even mentioning the possibility as far back as 1971. Let me just point out that he didn't actually do anything with the idea until 1979 [19]; in other words, the relational model managed perfectly well without nulls for some ten years.

LANGUAGE LEVELS

Before getting into details of ALPHA *per se,* reference [11] discusses the general question of language levels: "[Data] base systems may be classified by the data model with which the user interacts and the [level of] language provided to the user for expressing this interaction." The *data model* can be trees, nets, or relations; the *language level* can be low (Codd also calls this level "procedural"), intermediate (algebra-based), or high (calculus-based). Observe once again, therefore, that Codd is still treating the model and the operators as two different things. What's more (though the foregoing extract doesn't illustrate the point), he's also using the term "data model" once again to mean a model of the data *in a specific database,* instead of a model of data in general.

Before going any further, I should perhaps mention that some confusion exists over the term "procedural"; some people use it to mean what would more properly be described as *imperative.* While procedural languages will certainly be imperative, an imperative language might not be procedural. For example, we could certainly imagine a language that was based on Codd's relational algebra (and so nonprocedural) and yet was imperative in style.

Be that as it may, Codd goes on to consider the pros and cons of the three language levels and presents arguments to support his position that the calculus level is superior to the algebraic, which is in turn superior to the procedural. He notes, correctly, that these arguments "are particularly relevant to questions of intersystem compatibility and standardization"; he also notes that arguments already presented in reference [9] (regarding advantages of the relational model in general) reinforce those presented in this paper [11] in favor of both the calculus and algebraic levels over the procedural.

All in all, Codd's arguments in this section of the paper display a remarkable degree of foresight. Let me summarize those arguments here, very briefly.

- *Protection of users from representation clutter*

  "The provision of a conceptually concise model of the data and a powerful, conceptually concise language for its manipulation is not just an aesthetic concern. When users are forced to make numerous choices and decisions about avoidable representation details, the consequences are manifold and costly . . . This is not merely an argument for protecting users from . . . the sordid details of physical representation; it is an equally valid argument against imposing . . . an over-elaborate, conceptually redundant logical representation" (somewhat paraphrased). These arguments are as forceful, valid, and *correct* today as they were when they first appeared! How sad that our industry seems to have lost sight of them (I am, of course, thinking here of numerous recent attempts to replace the relational model by some kind of "object model").

- *Descriptive* vs. *constructive expression of intent*

  Here Codd characterizes the calculus as *descriptive* and the algebra as *constructive* (or *prescriptive*), and argues that the former is preferable to the latter. As noted in Chapter 5, I don't fully agree with this position—but I do certainly agree that (as Codd says) the calculus and the algebra are both superior to the procedural approach.

- *Understanding and modifying programs*

    This point is a corollary of the previous two. "Clarity of intent is important, [especially] when an application program has to be changed [and especially when that change has to be made by] people who did not write the program [in the first place]." In this connection, Codd invites us to compare the effort involved in changing the order of two quantifiers in an ALPHA program with the work needed to restructure a corresponding CODASYL program to achieve the same effect. Nice example!

- *Evolutionary development of search techniques*

    "Adoption of the calculus approach permits successive improvements in general search algorithms to be incorporated into data base systems without impacting user programs" (I would say the same is true of the algebraic approach, too). In other words, moving performance considerations out of user programs means those programs can *automatically* take advantage of evolutionary—even revolutionary—developments in physical data access technology.

- *Evolutionary development of data structures*

    This point is related to, and similar to, the previous one (it means that user programs can automatically take advantage of developments in physical storage technology too). *Note:* By "data structures" here, Codd really means *storage* structures.

- *Support for specialized query-update languages*

  "Many users need . . . languages specialized to their applications. The high cost of supporting [such] languages . . . suggests that [as much common functionality as possible] be identified and programmed once and for all . . . [Research on natural language query processors] suggests that the calculus-oriented language is an appropriate stepping-stone toward this goal." Again, all very true. Indeed, Codd's own later work on a natural language query system called Rendezvous [16] lent further weight to this particular argument.

CONCLUDING REMARKS

There are two final points I'd like to make to close out this discussion of Codd's ALPHA language.

1. The ALPHA paper mentions several planned follow-on papers: "[The present paper] is intended to provide a framework for subsequent papers on authorization principles, search tactics, and data representation techniques" (page 2). "Detailed treatment of [the catalog] will be postponed to another paper" (page 35). "Several additional features are desirable . . . [including] interlocking, access authorization, integrity preservation, virtual attributes, literal insertions . . . Various types of errors and . . . feedback [information]

... have ... been intentionally omitted. These aspects will be discussed in a later paper" (page 41). Sadly, I don't think any of these promised papers ever actually materialized!

2. Together with three colleagues, Codd subsequently worked on the design of a low-level subsystem called GAMMA-0, which was intended to serve as a basis for implementing higher-level relational languages like ALPHA [4]. More precisely, GAMMA-0 was intended as a basis for implementing another, slightly higher-level, interface called GAMMA-1, and GAMMA-1 in turn was intended as a basis for implementing truly high-level languages like ALPHA. The principal difference between GAMMA-0 and GAMMA-1 was that GAMMA-0 provided a single-user interface only, while GAMMA-1 provided a multi-user one. They were, of course, designed in concert: "Essential aspects of GAMMA-1 [were] considered and were influential in certain GAMMA-0 design choices" [4].

GAMMA-0 and GAMMA-1 together exhibit many points of similarity with the storage subsystem of System R [2] known as the RSS ("Relational Storage System"). It's therefore presumably not just coincidence that one of Codd's three coworkers on the GAMMA projects, Irv Traiger, was later the manager of the RSS project during much of its life.

Chapter 8

The First Three Normal Forms

Part 1 of 2

The beginnings of relational dependency theory

As if the invention of an entirely new theory of data (the relational model) wasn't contribution enough, Codd went on to use that theory as a basis for developing another completely new, and important, set of theoretical ideas: namely, the ideas of *further normalization*. The field of further normalization (now more usually referred to as *dependency theory,* though Codd himself didn't use that term) can be regarded as a separate discipline, one that sits on top of the relational model but is not itself part of that model. As is well known, the most obvious practical application of dependency theory is in database design, but its usefulness is certainly not limited to that area alone. In fact, the "dependencies" of dependency theory are really a special case of integrity constraints in general, and many of the ideas that were developed as part of dependency theory turned out to be relevant to other kinds of integrity constraints as well.

By the way, there's no truth in the story (so far as I know) that Codd introduced the terminology of "normalizing relations" because Richard Nixon was trying to "normalize relations" with China at the time Codd was doing his research.

THE NORMALIZATION PAPERS

Codd wrote three papers on the topic of further normalization. In chronological order, they are:

1. The Second and Third Normal Forms for the Relational Model [10]

2. Further Normalization of the Data Base Relational Model [12]

3. Normalized Data Base Structure: A Brief Tutorial [13]

The first of these papers [10], a brief (four-page) and rather terse technical memo, contains the first published definitions of second and third normal form—though it's worth noting that it defines those concepts in terms of *collections* of relations, not in terms of relations *per se:*

A collection *C* of relations is in *second normal form* if . . . every relation *R* in *C* [is in second normal form as we now understand that term] . . . A collection *C* of relations is in *third normal form* if . . . every relation *R* in *C* [is in third normal form as we now understand that term].

The other two papers, by contrast, frame their definitions and discussions in terms of individual relations, not collections of relations.

I remark without further comment that this first paper unfortunately continues to talk in terms of domains instead of attributes; it also continues to talk as if the phrase "the relational model" referred to a view of the data *in some specific database* (in fact, this latter criticism applies to the other two papers as well).

The second paper [12] is the most formal of the three, and the one I want to concentrate on in this chapter. It's really the primary source on the subject; indeed, it's often referred to, informally, just as "Codd's normalization paper." All quotes in what follows are taken from this paper unless otherwise indicated.

The third paper [13] is, as its title makes clear, primarily tutorial in nature. It concerns itself not so much with the higher normal forms *per se,* but rather with the idea that (a) relations in general can represent anything that other data structures—hierarchies, networks (here called "plexes"), and so on—can; moreover, (b) they do it better! ("[Users often have] occasion to require tables to be printed out or displayed. What could be a simpler, more universally needed, and more universally understood data structure than a table? Why not permit . . . users to view all the data . . . in a tabular way?") The paper does go on to discuss second and third normal forms briefly, but its coverage is essentially limited to giving a single—and *very* informal—example in each case.

Note: Like the relational completeness paper [15], the third paper [13] also—very unfortunately, in my opinion!—says that "each item [in a relation] is a simple number or a character string." As noted in Chapter 4, the misconception that relational systems are capable of dealing only with very simple data such as numbers and strings remains widespread to this day, and remarks such as the one just quoted must be held partly responsible for that misconception.

Incidentally, while I'm on the subject of what can go inside relations, I should mention that (oddly enough) the sole appearance of a definition of *first* normal form in any of the three papers [10,12,13] is tucked away in an appendix to reference [12]:

A relation is in *first normal form* if . . . none of its domains has elements which are themselves sets.
An *unnormalized relation* is one which is not in first normal form.

As noted in Chapter 3, I don't quite accept this definition, because I don't fully accept Codd's notion—implicit in the definition—of data value atomicity. However, I don't want to get into that particular discussion here; if you're interested, you can find more details in a paper by Hugh Darwen [24] or my book *An Introduction to Database Systems* [49].

One last point: The three papers [10,12,13] don't use the abbreviations 1NF, 2NF, 3NF; however, those abbreviations have since become virtually standard in the industry, and I'll use them myself in what follows.

ADVANTAGES OF FURTHER NORMALIZATION

Reference [12] gives the following list of advantages that accrue from adopting a level of normalization higher than just first. (Actually, the paper refers to these advantages as *objectives*—for further normalization, that is—rather than as advantages as such. Please note that I've reworded them all somewhat here.)

1. It frees the database from certain insert, update, and delete anomalies.
2. It reduces the need to restructure the database as new kinds of data are introduced, thereby increasing application lifetimes.
3. It makes the database more informative to users.
4. It avoids biasing the database design in favor of certain queries at the expense of others.

Subsequently, the paper suggests that an additional advantage is that "the [higher] normal forms . . . tend to capture some aspects of the semantics (minor, of course)." I love that parenthetical remark! What a contrast to some of the overblown claims we so often encounter elsewhere in the literature regarding "semantic modeling" and the like.

Note: The tutorial paper [13] mentions two further advantages of normalization (noting, however, that—unlike the ones already quoted—these two apply to mere *first* normal form rather than to 2NF and 3NF as such). Again I've paraphrased the original material somewhat:

5. It allows any relation to be represented as a table (basically because "all attribute values are atomic").

6. It allows the operations needed for data access to be simpler than they would otherwise have to be.

References [10] and [12] also both mention a couple of possible *dis*advantages of further normalization: "[It incurs] the penalty of extra relation names . . . [Also, some] queries will . . . need to employ more join terms than might otherwise be the case." However, they do also go on to say: "This potential burden . . . can be eased by [providing predefined views] for heavily used . . . queries."

MAJOR NEW CONCEPTS

Codd's normalization paper [12] includes the first published definitions of an impressive number of highly important concepts. I've listed those concepts below, with commentary in each case; I've omitted most of the definitions, however, because as a database professional you should be thoroughly familiar with them already.

- *Functional dependence*

   As Codd says, "[this concept] . . . is fundamental to . . . data base design." How true! *Note:* The concept was mentioned in reference [10] also (necessarily so), but was there called *internal* dependence. It wasn't mentioned at all in the tutorial paper [13]. By the way, along with the functional dependence concept as such, Codd introduced the (fairly obvious) idea of *dependency diagrams,* though he didn't actually use that term. And, of course, he also introduced the standard notation "$R.A \rightarrow R.B$". Here A and B are sets of attributes of relation R, and the notation is read "B is functionally dependent on A," or "A functionally determines B," in R. The notation can be simplified to just $A \rightarrow B$ if R is understood.

- *Full dependence*

  The functional dependence $A \rightarrow B$ is said to be *full* (and B is said to be *fully* dependent on A) if B isn't functionally dependent on any proper subset of A (remember that A and B are both *sets* of attributes). *Note:* "Full" isn't really the *mot juste* here; I prefer the term *irreducible* myself (but it's not a big deal). Reference [10] uses the term *minimal*.

- *Transitive dependence*

  I assume you know the meaning of this term. However, I should mention that Codd also defines what he calls *strict* transitive dependence: Given a relation R, $R.C$ is strictly transitively dependent on $R.A$ if there exists some $R.B$ such that $R.A \rightarrow R.B$ and $R.B \rightarrow R.C$ *and $R.C \nrightarrow R.B$ and $R.B \nrightarrow R.A$.* This concept is used in the definition of "optimal 3NF," which I'll discuss in the next chapter. *Note:* Reference [10] uses the term *immediate* in place of *nontransitive* (and, presumably, *nonimmediate* in place of *transitive*).

- *Trivial dependence*

  A functional dependence $A \rightarrow B$ is said to be *trivial* if the set of attributes B is a subset (not necessarily a proper subset) of the set of attributes A.

■ *Candidate key*

A candidate key K is required to be *unique* and *nonredundant* (the latter term means that no attribute can be discarded from K without destroying the uniqueness property; again I prefer the term *irreducible* for this concept, but again it's not a big deal). Codd makes the important observations that (a) each attribute of relation R is functionally dependent on each candidate key of R, and (b) within any given candidate key, no proper subset of the attributes is functionally dependent on any other.

Note: It follows immediately from the first of these two observations that each attribute of R is functionally dependent on each *superkey* of R. (A superkey is a superset—not necessarily a proper superset—of a candidate key; in other words, we can obtain a definition of "superkey" by simply dropping the irreducibility requirement from the definition of "candidate key.")

Codd then goes on to say: "For each relation R in a data base, one of its candidate keys is arbitrarily designated as the *primary* key of R. The usual [*sic!*] operational distinction . . . is that no tuple is allowed to have an undefined value for any of the primary key components, whereas . . . components of [other candidate keys] may have an undefined value. This restriction is imposed because of the vital role played by primary keys in search algorithms."

You might recall that Codd said something a little similar to the foregoing in his 1970 paper too [9]. Like many other people, I've always been a bit bothered by the fact that the primary key is chosen "arbitrarily"; indeed, I've argued elsewhere [35] that there are cases where we shouldn't have to choose a primary key at all (the only hard requirement is that we must have at least one *candidate* key). And I don't care very much for Codd's "usual operational distinction" between primary and nonprimary keys (as you probably know, that distinction—which was first mentioned, so far as I know, in the paper under discussion—was later elevated into the *entity integrity* rule [19]). Also, I have to say I'm a little suspicious of Codd's justification for that "usual distinction," which seems to me to smack of implementation concerns.

I note in passing that references [10] and [13] both talk in terms of primary keys only, not alternate keys (an alternate key is a candidate key that's not the primary key). That is, both papers make the tacit assumption that every relation has just one candidate key, which can thus be regarded, harmlessly, as the primary key. Indeed, Codd doesn't use the term "alternate key" at all; in fact, I think the term is probably due to me (not that I'm especially proud of it)—I introduced it in the third (1981) edition of my book *An Introduction to Database Systems* [49].

- *Insert / update / delete anomaly*

Actually it was the tutorial paper [13] that introduced the term "anomaly"—reference [12] used "dependency"—but "anomaly" is the term that's passed into general use. Neither term was formally defined, but the concept is so important that I felt it should be included in this list anyway. *Note:* Oddly enough, Codd nowhere points out explicitly that the anomalies in question are caused by *redundancy;* yet I know from my experience of teaching this material that when people first come to it, they immediately grasp the idea that low levels of normalization lead to redundancy (and "everyone knows" that redundancy is bad), whereas they have rather more difficulty in directly grasping the anomalies such redundancy can cause.

- *Second normal form*

    Here's Codd's definition of 2NF: A relation R is in second normal form if it's in first normal form and every nonprime attribute is fully dependent on each candidate key of R. (A prime attribute is an attribute that participates in at least one candidate key—not necessarily the primary key, despite the terminology!—of the relation in question; a nonprime attribute is, of course, one that isn't prime.)

    Now, what Codd was trying to do in introducing the prime attribute concept was head off an argument that said, for example, that the familiar shipments relation SP {S#,P#,QTY} wasn't in 2NF because attributes S# and P# weren't *fully* dependent on the candidate key {S#,P#}. As you probably know, however, the concepts did lead to some trouble later, especially in connection with *third* normal form (see below). I'll have more to say on this topic in the next chapter.

    Incidentally, reference [12] was the first paper to make explicit the important point that the further normalization process is, precisely, a process of taking *projections,* and further that we can recover the original relation by taking the *natural join* of those projections. In other words, the process is *reversible,* or—equivalently—the decomposition is *nonloss.* Note, therefore, that dependency theory involves all three aspects of the original relational model (structure, integrity, manipulation), not just the structural aspect alone.

Note: Reference [12] doesn't really discuss the actual *process* of further normalization in any detail. To be more specific, it doesn't explicitly spell out the general rules regarding which projections to take, nor does it offer any proof of reversibility. However, a first cut at such rules and such a proof appeared in a more or less contemporary—though much overlooked— paper by Ian Heath [54].

- *Third normal form*

  Again, here's Codd's definition: A relation R is in third normal form if it's in second normal form and every nonprime attribute is nontransitively dependent on each candidate key of R. Note again the reference to nonprime attributes. Again, I'll have more to say on this topic in the next chapter.

Chapter 9

The First Three Normal Forms

Part 2 of 2

Concluding our look at Codd's normalization ideas

In the previous chapter, I discussed Codd's groundbreaking definitions of *functional dependence, candidate key,* and *second* and *third normal forms* (2NF and 3NF). However, I did also note that the 3NF definition in particular wasn't entirely satisfactory in its original form, owing to its reliance on the concept of *nonprime attributes*. In this chapter, I'll explain this latter remark. First, however, I want to examine the concept of *optimal* normal forms.

OPTIMAL NORMAL FORMS

I noted in Chapter 8 that Codd's first paper on further normalization [10] defined 2NF and 3NF in terms of *collections* of relations. For example: "A collection *C* of relations is in *third normal form* if . . . every relation *R* in *C* [is in third normal form as we now understand that term]."

Now, this focus on collections is understandable, given that we often do seem to need a shorthand way of saying that (for instance) every relation in the database is in 3NF. The concept of *optimal normal form* addresses this issue, in part (though it also does more, as we'll see). Reference [12] defines two "optimal normal forms," optimal 2NF and optimal 3NF; both apply to *collections* of relations rather than to individual relations *per se*.

- *Optimal 2NF*

  A collection of relations is in *optimal 2NF* if (a) every relation in the collection is in 2NF and (b) the collection contains the fewest possible relations consistent with condition (a). In the case of the suppliers and parts database, for example, the usual collection of relations

  ```
  S  { S#, SNAME, STATUS, CITY }
  P  { P#, PNAME, COLOR, WEIGHT, CITY }
  SP { S#, P#, QTY }
  ```

  is in optimal 2NF. However, if we were to replace (say) relation S by its projections on {S#,SNAME, CITY} and {S#,STATUS}, the resulting collection would no longer be optimal. Loosely speaking, therefore, "optimal 2NF" just means: Don't break relations down too far.

  Note: There's no claim that optimal 2NF is unique in any sense; a given collection of relations might have several distinct optimal 2NF equivalents.

- *Optimal 3NF*

  Let *C2* be an optimal 2NF collection of relations, and let *C3* be a collection of 3NF relations derived from those in *C2* by taking suitable projections. *C3* is in *optimal 3NF relative to C2* if (a) no relation in *C3* has a pair of attributes *A* and *C* such that *C* is strictly transitively dependent on *A* in some relation in *C2* and (b) *C3* contains the fewest possible relations consistent with condition (a). (Perhaps I should remind you what it means for *C* to be strictly transitively dependent on *A*. Given a relation *R, C* is strictly transitively dependent on *A* in *R* if there exists some *B* in *R* such that $A \to B$ and $B \to C$ *and* $C \nrightarrow B$ and $B \nrightarrow A$.)

By way of example, suppose the suppliers relation S {S#,STATUS,CITY} satisfies the functional dependency CITY $\to$ STATUS (I ignore attribute SNAME for simplicity). This relation is in 2NF but not 3NF. Now consider the collection of relations

```
SS { S#, STATUS }
SC { S#, CITY }
```

This collection contains 3NF relations only; in fact, it contains the fewest possible number of such relations. But it's not in *optimal* 3NF: It violates condition (a) of the definition, because relation SS contains two attributes, STATUS and S#, such that STATUS is strictly transitively dependent on S# (via CITY) in the original 2NF relation S.

What Codd is getting at here with condition (a) is what later came to be known as *dependency preservation* [49]. The dependency CITY $\to$ STATUS has been lost in the decomposition into projections SS and SC. To put it another way, the trouble with the two projections SS and SC is that they're not *independent* [58]. By contrast, consider the following alternative decomposition:

```
SC { S#, CITY }
CS { CITY, STATUS }
```

Again both relations are in 3NF. This time, however, (a) the dependency CITY → STATUS has been preserved; (b) the two projections SC and CS are independent; and (c) the collection of relations is in optimal 3NF.

Note: Again, there's no claim that optimal 3NF is unique in any sense; a given database might have several distinct optimal 3NF equivalents.

PRIME ATTRIBUTES REVISITED

Now let's get back to the question of prime *vs.* nonprime attributes. Just to remind you, an attribute is said to be *prime* if it participates in at least one candidate key of the relation in which it appears. Let me also remind you of Codd's original definition of 3NF: Relation R is in 3NF if it's in 2NF and every nonprime attribute is nontransitively dependent on each candidate key of R.

Now let's take a look at an example (borrowed from reference [49]). Suppose every supplier has both a unique supplier name and a unique supplier number, and consider the following relation, SSP (an extended version of the usual shipments relation):

```
SSP { S#, SNAME, P#, QTY }
    CANDIDATE KEY { S#, P# }
    CANDIDATE KEY { SNAME, P# }
```

Now, relation SSP obviously suffers from certain redundancies (and is accordingly subject to certain update anomalies). To be specific, the fact that a given supplier has a certain supplier number and a certain supplier name appears many times in this relation, in general. Yet the relation is in 3NF according to Codd's definition! The problem is that Codd's definition requires only *nonprime* attributes to be fully dependent on every candidate key—and the redundancies in SSP are caused by the fact that certain *prime* attributes aren't fully dependent on certain candidate keys. (In terms of the definition shown above, we have S# → SNAME and SNAME → S#; hence S# isn't fully dependent on the second candidate key and SNAME isn't fully dependent on the first.)

So Codd's definition of 3NF still permitted certain redundancies (and hence certain update anomalies) to occur. In 1974, therefore, he presented an "improved definition of 3NF" (developed with Raymond Boyce) that took care of this problem [18]. However, that new definition was strictly stronger than the old one, in the sense that every relation that satisfies the new definition also satisfies the old, but some relations satisfy the old one and not the new. Thus, it doesn't really make sense to say that the new definition defines "3NF" *per se;* instead, we now say it defines *Boyce/Codd normal form* (BCNF). A discussion of BCNF can be found in reference [44].

Note: Actually, a definition of "third" normal form that was equivalent to the BCNF definition was first given by Ian Heath in 1971 [54]. "Heath normal form" might thus have been a more fitting name than BCNF.

Incidentally, this slight confusion over 3NF and BCNF was cleared up very elegantly in a paper by Carlo Zaniolo [61]. First, Zaniolo gave this definition of 3NF:

- Let R be a relation, let X be any set of attributes of R, and let A be any single attribute of R. Then R is in 3NF if and only if, for every functional dependency $X \to A$ in R, at least one of the following is true:
  1. X contains A;
  2. X contains a candidate key of R;
  3. A is contained in a candidate key of R.

Explanation: Possibility 1 takes care of trivial dependencies (trivial dependencies are *always* satisfied and can never be eliminated). Possibility 2 takes care of dependencies implied by superkeys (as we saw in Chapter 8, if X is a superkey, then $X \to A$ is true for all attributes A; these dependencies too are always satisfied and can never be eliminated). Possibility 3 corresponds to that part of Codd's definition that allows *prime* attributes not to be "fully" (irreducibly) dependent on each candidate key.

Next, Zaniolo's definition of BCNF is obtained from his 3NF definition by simply dropping possibility 3. Among other things, this definition has the virtue that it shows immediately that BCNF is strictly stronger than 3NF. In fact, of course, when people talk informally of "3NF," it's usually BCNF that they really have in mind.

THE SJT EXAMPLE

There's another example I want to mention briefly (this one is taken from reference [49] also; I discussed it in some detail in reference [45]). We're given relation SJT {S,J,T}, where S, J, and T stand for student, subject, and teacher, respectively; the meaning of row (s,j,t) is that student s is taught subject j by teacher t. We're also told that the following functional dependencies hold:

```
{ S, J } → T
```

(for each subject, each student of that subject is taught by only one teacher);

```
T → J
```

(each teacher teaches only one subject).

Like relation SSP from the previous section, relation SJT is in 3NF but not BCNF, and so we should probably break it down (it certainly involves redundancy in its present form, and it's certainly subject to update anomalies of various kinds). As I've pointed out elsewhere, however (see, e.g., reference [45]), breaking it down necessarily violates the objective—mentioned briefly in the section on optimal normal forms—of dependency preservation. It follows that the two objectives of *avoiding update anomalies* and *preserving dependencies* are sometimes in conflict with each other; that is, it isn't always possible to achieve both objectives simultaneously.

The reason I mention this example is that—to his credit—Codd was already aware of this problem in 1971! He expresses it differently, though, saying that "[it] is not always possible to remove *all* transitive dependencies without losing information." In terms of the SJT example, he would say that J is transitively dependent on the candidate key {S,J}. Of course, J is also *trivially* dependent on that candidate key, so it's a little difficult to see what he's really getting at here, but what he means is that breaking SJT down into its two BCNF projections on

{S,T} and {T,J}—which is what the further normalization discipline would suggest—loses the functional dependency {S,J} → T.

CONCLUDING REMARKS

If we accept the rule that no tuple can have an undefined value for any primary key component, then, as reference [12] points out, a database in which all relations are in 3NF is capable of representing certain information that an otherwise equivalent database in which all relations are only in 2NF isn't. An analogous remark holds if we replace 2NF by 1NF and 3NF by 2NF, of course. These facts can be seen as additional advantages of 3NF over 2NF and 2NF over 1NF.

Further, Codd adds: "It is also conjectured that *physical* records in optimal 3NF will prove to be highly economical in [storage] space" (my italics). "In some cases, a further saving in space can be obtained by factoring" (I discussed the operation of factoring, or *nesting,* in Chapter 4).

Reference [12] concludes with a brief discussion of growth and restructuring in the database, including in particular a look at the question of "attribute migration" (see Chapter 7). "It is this author's thesis that, by casting [all relations in] the data base in third normal form at the earliest possible time . . . an installation will reduce the incidence of attribute migration to a minimum, and consequently have less trouble keeping its application programs in a viable state." Quite right.

Chapter 10

Relational Really Is Different

An analysis of Codd's contribution to the Great Debate

The *Great Debate* was a debate between proponents of the relational and network approaches. It was held at the ACM SIGMOD Workshop on Data Description, Access, and Control in 1974; the principal speakers were Edgar F. Codd for the relational approach (surprise!) and Charles W. Bachman for the network or CODASYL approach. In preparing for the debate, Codd wrote a paper entitled "Interactive Support for Nonprogrammers: The Relational and Network Approaches" [17], and it's that paper that I want to discuss in the present chapter.

Note: The paper is shown in the debate proceedings as being a joint production by Codd and myself; in fact, however, it was wholly written by Codd. (The companion paper [50], on application programming considerations, which is also attributed to both of us, was written by myself, and isn't at all of the same caliber.)

OVERVIEW OF THE PAPER

Of course, the battle between relations and networks is ancient history now (the good guys won). This fact notwithstanding, Codd's paper—even though it was written over 25 years ago—is still worth reading today as a beautiful example of *clear thinking*. Indeed, it's quite remarkable to see how, on a topic where *muddled* thinking was the norm at the time, Codd was able to do such a good job of cutting to the chase and focusing on the real issues. Let me elaborate:

- First of all, Codd realized that to compare the very concrete CODASYL specifications and the much more abstract relational model would be an apples-and-oranges comparison and would involve numerous distracting irrelevancies.

- Hence, it would be necessary *first* to define an abstract "network model." The comparison could then be done on a level playing field, as it were, in a fair and sensible manner.

- Codd therefore proceeded to define an abstraction of the CODASYL specifications that might reasonably be regarded as such a model (and then, of course, he went on to compare that abstraction with the relational model).

Thus, Codd has some claim to being the first person anywhere to attempt to give an abstract definition, not just of the relational model (of course), but also of a *network* model! Certainly none of the original CODASYL documents ever attempted any such thing.

(In fact, reference [17] might still be timely after all, even though the original battle is over. Certainly we are—regrettably!—seeing some of the same tired old issues surfacing again in connection with object DBMSs. As several writers have observed, object DBMSs do tend to look like "CODASYL warmed over" in certain respects. A case of those who don't know history being doomed to repeat it?)

Anyway, the most significant contribution in Codd's paper is probably his introduction of the concept of *essentiality,* a concept that's critical to a proper understanding of data models in general and relations *vs.* networks in particular. It's the concept of essentiality that allows us to pinpoint the crucial difference between relational databases and others, as we'll see in the next section. Indeed, the concept of essentiality is really the main reason I want to talk about the paper [17] at all.

As well as introducing the essentiality notion, reference [17] also raises a number of pertinent questions regarding the suitability of network structures as a component of what it calls "the principal schema"—questions that, so far as I know, have never been answered in the open literature. To quote: "In the past, many designers of software systems . . . have confused two quite distinct notions: enrichment of features on the one hand, and generality of application on the other." How true! "A crucial issue in database management systems is that of the richness (that is, variety) of data structures . . . that should be supported in the principal schema. In the event that enrichment of these data structures . . . beyond the minimum is proposed, we ask the following questions . . ." (I don't want to discuss the questions themselves in detail here, however, since I've already considered them at some length elsewhere [30]).

Incidentally, the foregoing quote reminds me of another one, which appeared in Codd's tutorial paper on normalization [13]: "Several existing systems permit a variety of physical representations for a given logical structure . . . The complexity of the physical representations which these systems support is, perhaps, understandable, because these representations are selected in order to obtain high performance . . . What is less understandable is the trend toward more and more complexity in the data structures with which . . . users directly interact. Surely, in the choice of logical data structures that a system is to support, there is one consideration that is of *absolutely paramount importance—*and that is the convenience of the majority of users." Again, how true!

Back to reference [17]. The paper also includes an appendix comparing CODASYL/COBOL and relational/ALPHA versions of a simple machine shop scheduling application. That comparison provides strong evidence in support of relational claims of *simplicity* (simplicity for the user, that is). For full details of the comparison, including the actual code used in the two solutions, I refer you to the original paper [17]; here I content myself with simply repeating a few remarks from an earlier paper of my own [29] that discusses the same example. Here are a few comparative statistics:

	CODASYL	*relational*
GO TO	15	0
PERFORM UNTIL	1	0
currency indicators	10	0
IF	12	0
FIND	9	0
GET	4	1
STORE / PUT	2	1
MODIFY	1	0
MOVE CURRENCY	4	0
other MOVEs	9	1
SUPPRESS CURRENCY	4	0
total statements	>60	3

The relative simplicity of the relational solution is very striking. *Note:* In fact, the relational solution could have been reduced to just a single statement, a PUT; the GET and MOVE aren't strictly necessary. What's more (although Codd doesn't mention the fact in reference [17]), the CODASYL "solution"—which was taken from another source, by the way, not created by Codd himself—included at least two *bugs!*

The example highlights another point, too. To quote Codd [17]: "The reader is cautioned to avoid comparing [different] approaches *solely* on the basis of differences in [data structure]. An adequate appreciation of the differences . . . must entail consideration of the . . . operators also." And later he adds: "Discussions on the relational approach often become riveted on the [data structure] component to the neglect of [other components]. To do justice to this approach, all . . . components must be considered as a package."

ESSENTIALITY

Although this concept is so important, it's my experience that few database professionals are really familiar with it. The discussion that follows therefore has more of a tutorial flavor than most of the discussions in earlier chapters have done. *Note:* The material that follows is based in part on another earlier paper of mine [39].

First of all, "everyone knows" that the only data structure available in the relational model is the relation itself. To understand the significance of this point, however, it's necessary to know something about at least one other data structure: for example, the *link* structure found in hierarchic and network systems. So let's look at an example. Fig. 10.1 shows (a) the relational design for

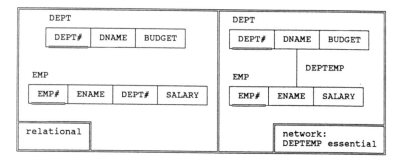

Fig. 10.1   Departments and employees: relational and
network designs

a simple departments and employees database, together with (b) a network equivalent of that design. (Actually, the example is so simple that the network design degenerates to a mere *hierarchy,* but that point's not important for present purposes. Hierarchies and networks are much more like each other than either one is like relations.)

The network design involves a "CODASYL set" (not to be confused with a mathematical set—the two concepts are quite different). Each *occurrence* of that CODASYL set consists of a DEPT row, a set of corresponding EMP rows, and an occurrence of a *link* ("DEPTEMP") that connects those DEPT and EMP rows together. (I use the term "row" here rather than the more usual "record" in order to avoid distractions caused by mere terminological differences between the two approaches.) Within a given CODASYL set occurrence, the corresponding link occurrence can be thought of as *a chain of pointers*—a pointer from the DEPT row to the first EMP row for that DEPT, a pointer from that EMP row to the next for the same DEPT, and so on, and finally a pointer from the last EMP row back to the original DEPT. *Note:* Those "pointers" needn't be physically represented in storage by actual pointers, but the user can always *think* of them as actual pointers (that's the network model).

Observe now that the EMP rows in the network design don't include a DEPT# column. Thus, to find what department a given employee is in, we have to traverse the DEPTEMP link occurrence from the applicable EMP row to the corresponding DEPT row; likewise, to find the employees in a given department, we have to traverse the DEPTEMP link occurrence from the applicable DEPT row to the corresponding EMP rows. In other words, the information that was represented by a *foreign key* in the relational design is represented by a *link* in the network design; links are the network analog of foreign keys (speaking *very* loosely).

Now let's consider a couple of queries against this database. For each query, I'll show a relational (SQL) formulation and a network equivalent, using a hypothetically extended version of SQL that caters for links.

Q1: Get employee numbers and employee names for employees with salary greater than 20K.

Relational: *Network:*

```
SELECT  EMP#, ENAME        SELECT  EMP#, ENAME
FROM    EMP                FROM    EMP
WHERE   SALARY > 20K ;     WHERE   SALARY > 20K ;
```

Q2: Get employee numbers and employee names for employees with salary greater than 20K in department D3.

Relational: *Network:*

```
SELECT  EMP#, ENAME        SELECT  EMP#, ENAME
FROM    EMP                FROM    EMP
WHERE   SALARY > 20K       WHERE   SALARY > 20K
AND     DEPT# = 'D3' ;     AND   ( SELECT  DEPT#
                                   FROM    DEPT
                                   OVER    EMP ) = 'D3' ;
```

For query Q1 the two formulations are obviously identical; for query Q2, however, they're not. The relational formulation for Q2 still has the same basic form as for Q1 (SELECT–FROM–WHERE, with a simple restriction condition in the WHERE clause); the network formulation, by contrast, has to use *a new language construct,* the OVER clause (which is my hypothetical SQL representation of a link-traversing operation). The

WHERE condition in that formulation is certainly not a simple restriction condition.

Query Q2 thus illustrates the important point that networks *fundamentally require* certain additional data access operators. Note too that those operators *are* additional; the relational operators are still needed as well, as query Q1 shows. Note moreover that this point applies not only to *all* of the data manipulation operators (update operators included), but also to the *definitional* operators, the *security* operators, the *integrity* operators, and so on. The links of the network data structure thus certainly add *complexity*. However, they don't add any *power*—there's nothing that can be represented by a network that can't be represented by relations, and there's no query that can be answered from a network and not from relations.

Now, it's sometimes suggested that the complexity can be reduced by reinstating the DEPT# component (the foreign key) in EMP, as shown in Fig. 10.2. This redesign allows query Q2 (network version) to be formulated without using the OVER construct; in fact, the formulation

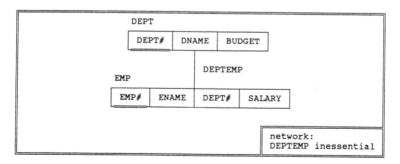

Fig. 10.2 Departments and employees: network design with foreign key EMP.DEPT# reinstated

becomes identical to its relational counterpart. The reason is, of course, that DEPT and EMP in that revised design are identical to their relational analogs; the database is now identical to its relational equivalent, except for the DEPTEMP link. However, that link is *wholly redundant*—it doesn't represent any information that isn't also represented by the foreign key, and we can therefore ignore it without losing any logical functionality.

So now (at last!) I can explain the notion of *essentiality*. A data construct is *essential* if its loss would cause a loss of information—by which I mean, very precisely, that *some relation would no longer be derivable*. For example, in the relational version of departments and employees, all data constructs (all rows and all columns) are essential in this sense. Likewise, in the original network version (Fig. 10.1), all data constructs (all rows, all columns, and all links) are again essential. But in the revised network of Fig. 10.2, the rows and columns are essential *but the link is inessential*. There's no information that can be derived from that network that can't be derived from the rows and columns alone; there's no logical need for the link at all.

Note: Some people might argue that the opposite is the case—the link is essential and the foreign key is inessential. But that argument misses the point, which is that, since some rows and columns *must* be essential, and nothing else need be, then why have anything else?

Now (finally) I can pin down the crucial difference between a relational database and any other kind, say a network database. In a relational database, the *only* essential data construct is the relation itself. In other databases, *there must be at least one additional essential data construct* (typically an essential link). For if there isn't, then the database is really a relational database that happens to have certain access paths exposed (and there's no requirement that the user use those access paths, and the question arises as to why they're exposed anyway when others aren't). And it's those additional essential data constructs that lead to much (not all) of the complexity of nonrelational databases.

Note: In the case of CODASYL specifically, there are at least four additional constructs that can also be used to carry information essentially. To get into details of those other constructs here would take us much too far afield, however.

A NOTE ON ORDERING

The concept of essentiality allows me to explain why it's significant that relations have no ordering to their rows. In an ordered file, the ordering itself might be essential in the sense explained above. For example, a file of temperature readings might be kept in the order in which those readings were taken; the ordering itself might thus carry information, which would be lost if the records of the file were rearranged—just as information can be lost if someone drops a box of cards, if those cards don't include a sequence field. (If you're too young to know what boxes of cards and sequence fields are all about, then I envy you, and you can ignore this example!) And essential ordering, like an essential link, requires additional operators to deal with it—"find the nth record," "insert a record between records n and $n+1$," and so on. For this reason it's not permitted in the relational model.

In contrast to the foregoing, it's sometimes suggested that *in*essential ordering might be acceptable. A file is inessentially ordered if it's ordered on the basis of the value(s) of some field(s); for example, the employee file might be ordered by employee number, but no information would be lost if the records were shuffled around. Some "relational" systems do in fact support ordering in this sense. Note, however, that relations *per se* are unordered by definition; it would really be better to regard an "ordered relation" as a totally different kind of thing—perhaps as, precisely, a sequential file. In this regard, the SQL ORDER BY operation might best be thought of as converting a relation into such a file, rather than as "ordering a relation."

In any case, even inessential data constructs can cause problems, because they do still carry information, even though they're inessential. For example, they might represent a *security* exposure. Suppose a file of employee records is ordered, inessentially, by increasing salary. Then the fact that your manager's record appears in the file after your own certainly tells you something, even if you're not authorized to see actual salary values.

CONCLUDING REMARKS

In conclusion, let me get back to Codd's "great debate" paper [17]. Codd observes, wisely, that it's "not enough to take note of where [the] approaches stand today—we must also be clear about where they're going." He contends that "casual" users of database systems will become increasingly important (in fact, they'll soon be the largest user constituency of all), and so we must pay attention to what the different approaches are or might be doing to support such users. Some quotes:

- "Such users clearly need a simple logical notion of the data organization in order to frame their queries or modifications in a simple way."

- "The absence in the network approach of operators at the algebraic or calculus level is noteworthy, since such operators play a vital role in supporting [casual user] interaction . . . [Indeed, the] absence from the [CODASYL proposals] of any specific objectives for the support of nonprogrammer interaction is especially noteworthy."

- "General-purpose support for such users entails provision of an *augmented, relationally complete, retrieval capability* without branching, explicit iteration, or cursors. It's clear how this capability can be realized with the relational approach—whether with a formal or informal language interface. It's not at all clear how the network approach can reach this goal, so long as the principal schema includes [CODASYL sets] bearing information essentially." *Note:* The "augmentation" Codd had in mind here had to do with the availability of library functions for counting, summing, and so on.

These observations need only minor changes in wording for them to be still highly pertinent today.

Chapter 11

Extending the Relational Model

When's an extension not an extension?

Ever since its inception, the relational model has been the target of an unusually high degree of criticism. To be more specific, many claims have been made over the years to the effect that (a) the model is seriously deficient in some respect or another, and accordingly (b) it therefore needs to be extended in some way or another. In this chapter, I want to examine this business of "extending the relational model" in some detail; in particular, I want to take a brief look at Codd's own extended version known as RM/T.

BOGUS *VS.* GENUINE EXTENSIONS

Some claims of deficiency in the model are valid, others aren't. As a consequence, some proposed extensions to the model are *genuine,* meaning that they do truly serve to add useful functionality; others, however, are *bogus,*

meaning either (a) that they don't add any new functionality or (b) that the functionality they do add isn't useful.
Examples of *genuine* extensions include such things as
the EXTEND and SUMMARIZE operators, the relational
comparison operators, and view updatability theory (I'm
sure we can agree that these examples all do provide useful new functionality). Examples of *bogus* extensions include such things as quota queries, date and time
support, and "data of type REF" (REF = reference). Let
me immediately elaborate:

- Quota queries are certainly useful from a pragmatic
  point of view, but—at least as described in reference
  [43]—they're essentially just syntactic shorthand for
  functionality that already exists. Note carefully,
  therefore, that when I say an extension is bogus, I
  don't necessarily mean it's a bad thing; I just mean it
  isn't really an extension to the *model* as such.

- Date and time support is also useful. Furthermore, it
  isn't just a syntactic shorthand for something that already exists—it really does provide new functionality. However, it still isn't an extension to the *model,*
  since the question of what data types are supported is
  nothing to with the model ("types are orthogonal to
  tables" [25,52]).

- By contrast, "data of type REF" is bogus because it
  isn't useful!—indeed, it essentially drags back into
  the model all of the pointers and their associated bag-
  gage that Codd deliberately threw out, for very good
  reasons, all those years ago. (See reference [48] for a
  detailed discussion of this issue.)

Bogus extensions—when they're actually claimed to *be* extensions as such—tend to be predicated on a flawed understanding of the true nature of the model. The SQL community is especially at fault here, of course; SQL's many problems are ascribed to "relational model deficiencies," and solutions to those problems are then described as "relational model extensions." (As I've written elsewhere, many times, the biggest problem with SQL is precisely that it doesn't support the relational model!) The most recent, and perhaps most egregious, case in point is provided by the so-called *object / relational model,* which I'll discuss briefly in the next section.

"THE OBJECT/RELATIONAL MODEL"

Several SQL vendors have attempted (with varying degrees of success, I might add) to extend their SQL products to incorporate some kind of object functionality. They then go on to claim that their extended products thus support an "extended" version of the relational model, which they refer to as "the object/relational model" ("the O/R model" for short).

But this claim is absurd! As Hugh Darwen and I have shown in *The Third Manifesto* [25,52], object functionality and the relational model are completely orthogonal to one another. To quote: "The relational model needs no *extension,* no *correction,* no *subsumption,* and above all no *perversion,* in order [to achieve object functionality]." All that's needed is to support relational *domains* properly (which SQL never did), recognizing those domains for what they are, which is basically just *abstract data types* (ADTs), With All That That Entails. In other words, the so-called "O/R model" is just the relational model, pure and simple; there aren't any (genuine) "relational model extensions" involved at all.

THE RM/T PAPER: BASICS

Let's turn to some interesting genuine extensions to the model. In 1979, Codd published yet another important paper, this one entitled "Extending the Database Relational Model to Capture More Meaning" [19]. I'll refer to this paper as *the RM/T paper,* for reasons that will quickly become obvious. As the title suggests, the primary purpose of the RM/T paper was to suggest a set of "semantic" extensions to the original model; however, it began by summarizing the *basic* model (as of 1979), and I'd like to make a few remarks in that connection first before getting into details on the proposed extensions.

First of all, I believe I'm right in saying that the RM/T paper was actually the first of Codd's papers to include an explicit definition of the term *relational model!* Here is that definition:

"The relational model consists of

1. A collection of time-varying tabular relations (with the properties cited above—note especially the keys and domains);

2. The insert-update-delete rules (Rules 1 and 2 cited above);

3. The relational algebra described . . . below."

Aside: I do have a few comments on this definition, as follows:

- It's probably not a big deal, but to me it seems a little odd to say that the relational model includes "a collection of . . . relations" (a collection of relations is surely just a database?). I would have said rather that the model includes a *type generator* called RELATION, which allows users to define relation values and variables (*relation variables* [25,52], of course, being my preferred term for Codd's "time-varying tabular relations").

- "Rules 1 and 2 cited above" are the *entity integrity* and *referential integrity* rules. These rules were implicit, more or less, in earlier papers but hadn't previously been spelled out (or named, come to that). *Note:* As a matter of fact, the referential integrity rule was slightly defective as stated, inasmuch as it overlooked the possibility that foreign keys in general were supposed to permit nulls. Of course, the point is unimportant if you believe, as I do, that nulls should never have been introduced in the first place.

- The relational algebra "described . . . below" consists of the usual operators, together with some additional ones for dealing with "null values" [*sic*]. The paper defines the following such additional operators: MAYBE θ-JOIN, MAYBE DIVIDE, OUTER θ-JOIN, OUTER NATURAL JOIN, and OUTER UNION ("in a similar

manner, we could define OUTER versions of INTER-
SECTION and DIFFERENCE also"). This list of
operators raises many questions—for example, questions of orthogonality and completeness—but again I
don't think those questions are very important, since
I believe nulls and everything to do with them to be a
mistake (in my opinion Codd's one big error of judg-
ment in this whole business).

End of aside.

The RM/T paper was also the first by Codd to make
explicit mention of the idea of *relational assignment.*
However, the mention occurs only in connection with the
proposed semantic extensions; it isn't part of the "basic
relational model" definition given above, though it's certainly part of that model as now commonly understood.
Moreover, there's no discussion of the fact that INSERT,
UPDATE, and DELETE are basically just shorthand for
certain relational assignments.

Third, the paper also has this to say: "Closely associated with the relational model are various [semantic] concepts . . . Examples are . . . nonloss (natural) joins and
functional dependencies, multivalued dependencies, and
normal forms." Here, then, we have a clear statement of
Codd's position that these matters are to be seen as separate from (but "associated with") the model *per se*—
though I think he might subsequently have changed his
mind on this point [23].

Fourth, the RM/T paper was also the first in which
Codd embraced the idea of *surrogates*—meaning, essentially, system-assigned identifiers. (Again the concept is

brought in only in connection with the proposed semantic extensions, but there's no reason why it can't be used with the basic model, and indeed there are often good arguments in favor of doing so.) Unfortunately, however, the paper states that surrogates must be hidden from users—a clear violation of the paper's own earlier definition of a relational database, which says, to paraphrase, that all data in the database must be accessible to (authorized) users. In fact, hiding surrogates constitutes a clear violation of Codd's own *Information Principle,* which states that *all information in the database must be cast explicitly in terms of values in relations and in no other way.*

(Just as an aside, let me remind you that—as we saw in the previous chapter—relations *per se* are the only essential data construct allowed in a relational database. If I now add that relations are the only allowable *in*essential construct as well, then what we wind up with is effectively a statement of the *Information Principle.*)

Finally, the RM/T paper devotes a brief (too brief) section to the relationship between the relational model and predicate logic: "A database [is] a set of [propositions] in first-order predicate logic . . . [We can] factor out the predicate common to a set of simple [propositions] and then treat the [propositions] as an . . . *n*-ary relation and the predicate as the name of the relation." Codd goes on to refer to the "propositions" portion of the database as the *extension* and the "predicates" portion as the *intension* (extension and intension here being technical terms from logic). "One may . . . view the intension as a set of integrity constraints." And he briefly discusses the closed *vs.* open world interpretations. (Under the closed inter-

pretation, the omission of a given row from a given relation means the corresponding proposition is *false;* under
the open interpretation, it means we don't know whether
it's *true* or *false*.)

THE RM/T PAPER: EXTENSIONS

As I've already indicated, the bulk of reference [19] is concerned with an extended version of the relational model
called RM/T ("T for Tasmania, where these ideas were
first presented"). It opens with some nice preliminary remarks on the matter of semantic extensions and "semantic data modeling" in general:

- "Actually, the task of capturing the meaning of data is
  a never-ending one. So the label 'semantic' must not
  be interpreted in any absolute sense. Moreover, database models developed earlier (and sometimes attacked as 'syntactic') were not devoid of semantic
  features (take domains, keys, and functional dependence, for example). The goal [of semantic modeling]
  is nevertheless an extremely important one, because
  even small successes can bring understanding and
  order into the field of database design."

(What a pleasing contrast to the exaggerated claims so
often encountered in the semantic modeling field!) Later,
Codd makes another good point:

- "In recent papers on semantic data modeling there is
  a strong emphasis on structural aspects, sometimes to
  the detriment of manipulative aspects. Structure

without corresponding operators or inferencing techniques is rather like anatomy without physiology."

Nice analogy!

To turn now to RM/T specifically: RM/T generally falls into the same broad category as the rather better known "entity/relationship model" (E/R model for short) [5]. Even if never implemented, therefore (and to my knowledge it never has been), it can still serve—just as the E/R model can—as the basis for a systematic database design methodology. In fact, I personally prefer it to the E/R model for this purpose, since I find it to be more precisely specified. Some immediate differences between the two are as follows.

1. RM/T makes no unnecessary distinctions between entities and relationships—a relationship is regarded merely as a special kind of entity.

2. The structural and integrity aspects of RM/T are more extensive, and more precisely defined, than those of the E/R model.

3. RM/T includes its own special operators, over and above the operators of the basic relational model (though much additional work remains to be done in this last area).

In outline, RM/T works as follows:

1. Entities (including "relationships") are represented by *E-relations* and *P-relations,* both of which are special forms of the general *n*-ary relation. E-relations are used to record the fact that certain entities exist, P-relations are used to record certain properties of those

entities (E-relations are of degree exactly one, P-relations of degree at least two).

2. A variety of relationships can exist among entities; for example, entity types *A* and *B* might be linked together in an *association* (RM/T's term for a many-to-many relationship), or entity type *Y* might be a *subtype* of entity type *X*. RM/T includes a formal *catalog* structure by which such relationships can be made known to the system. The system is thus capable of enforcing the various *integrity constraints* that are implied by the existence of such relationships.

3. As already mentioned, a number of high-level *operators* are provided to facilitate the manipulation of the various RM/T objects (E-relations, P-relations, catalog relations, and so forth).

RM/T also provides an *entity classification scheme,* which in many respects constitutes the most significant aspect (or, at least, the most immediately visible aspect) of the entire model. To be more specific, entities are classified—though only informally, please note—into three categories, called *kernels, characteristics,* and *associations:*

- *Kernels:* Kernel entities are entities that have *independent existence;* they are "what the database is really all about." In other words, kernels are entities that are neither characteristic nor associative (see below). Examples might be suppliers and parts (but not shipments) in the usual suppliers and parts database.

- *Characteristics:* A characteristic entity is an entity whose primary purpose is to describe or "characterize" some other entity. An example might be individual line items on a customer order. Characteristics are *existence-dependent* on the entity they describe. The entity described can be kernel, characteristic, or associative.

- *Associations:* An associative entity is an entity whose function is to represent a *many-to-many* (or many-to-many-to-many . . .) *relationship* among two or more other entities. Shipments in the familiar suppliers and parts database provide an example. The entities associated can each be kernel, characteristic, or associative.

In addition:

- Entities (regardless of their classification) can also have *properties;* for example, parts have colors, line items have costs, shipments have quantities.

- In particular, any entity (again, regardless of its classification) can have a property whose function is to *designate* some other related entity; for example, orders designate customers. A designation represents a many-to-one relationship between two entities. *Note:* Actually, the idea of designations was added later [40]—it wasn't included in the original RM/T paper.

- Entity *supertypes* and *subtypes* are supported. If *B* is a subtype of *A,* then *B* is a kernel, a characteristic, or an association depending on whether *A* is a kernel, a characteristic, or an association. *Note:* The RM/T paper had virtually nothing to say on the related (and important!) notion of *inheritance,* however. Indeed, RM/T's notion of supertypes and subtypes has more to do with the somewhat suspect notion, now supported by the SQL standard [51], of "supertables and subtables" than it does with true type inheritance as discussed in, for example, *The Third Manifesto* [52].

The foregoing concepts can be related (somewhat loosely) to their E/R analogs as follows: A kernel corresponds to an E/R "regular entity"; a characteristic to an E/R "weak entity"; and an association to an E/R "relationship" (many-to-many variety only).

Note: In addition to the aspects discussed briefly above, RM/T also includes support for (a) the *time* dimension and (b) various kinds of *data aggregation*. For more detailed discussions, see Codd's original paper [19] or my own tutorial description of RM/T [40].

Chapter 12

Relational Forever!

The relational model will stand the test of time

I've now devoted eleven chapters to a historical review and analysis of Codd's original relational papers (or at least the most important of those papers). To be specific, I've examined the following papers in some detail:

- Derivability, Redundancy, and Consistency of Relations Stored in Large Data Banks [7]
- A Relational Model of Data for Large Shared Data Banks [9]
- A Data Base Sublanguage Founded on the Relational Calculus [11]
- Further Normalization of the Data Base Relational Model [12]
- Relational Completeness of Data Base Sublanguages [15]
- Interactive Support for Nonprogrammers: The Relational and Network Approaches [17]
- Extending the Database Relational Model to Capture More Meaning [19]

I've also briefly touched on a few other papers from time to time.

The time has come to start to bring these discussions to a close. In this final chapter, I'd like to set out some specific objectives for the relational model and consider how well it meets them (or doesn't meet them). I'd also like to take a brief look at exactly what the model is and where it might be headed. All in all, I'd like this whole series of discussions and commentary to be seen as a tribute to Codd's tremendous achievement in founding, more or less singlehanded, pretty much the entire field of modern database management—the field in which we all toil and from which we all obtain our livelihood. Thank you, Ted!

RELATIONAL OBJECTIVES

Let's begin by taking a look at what Codd himself thought he was trying to achieve with his relational research. It turns out, unsurprisingly, that several of his papers do address this issue. For example, in the RM/T paper [19], he says: "The relational model . . . was conceived . . . primarily as a tool to free users from the frustrations of having to deal with the clutter of storage representation details." More specifically, in the ALPHA paper [11], he identifies the following as "principal motivations of the relational model":

1. Data independence;
2. The simplest possible [data] structure consistent with semantic considerations;

3. Provision of a unifying principle which would simplify (a) the language needed for interaction and (b) statement analysis needed for authorization of access and optimization of search;

4. Relatively easy analysis for [data] consistency.

Later, in his "Great Debate" paper [17], he says: "The relational approach was developed as a response to the following requirements, which were considered to be relatively novel in 1968":

1. Data independence;

2. Integration of files into data bases;

3. Multiple user types;

4. Many online users at terminals;

5. Increased dynamic sharing of data;

6. Networks of mutually remote databases.

In an invited paper to the 1974 IFIP Congress [18]—the same year as the Great Debate—he lists the following as "the objectives of [the relational approach]":

1. To provide a high degree of data independence;

2. To provide a community view of the data of spartan simplicity, so that a wide variety of users in an enterprise (ranging from the most computer-naïve to the most computer-sophisticated) can interact with a *common* model (while not prohibiting superimposed user views for specialized purposes);

3. To simplify the potentially formidable job of the data base administrator;

4. To introduce a theoretical foundation (albeit modest) into data base management (a field sadly lacking in solid principles and guidelines);

5. To merge the fact retrieval and file management fields in preparation for the addition at a later time of inferential services in the commercial world;

6. To lift data-based application programming to a new level—a level in which sets (and more specifically relations) are treated as operands instead of being processed element by element.

And he adds: "In connection with the second [of these objectives], it is important to remember that data bases are being established for the benefits of end users, and not for the application programmers who act as middlemen [*sic*] for today's data processing needs."

Codd went on to repeat these same objectives in the Great Debate paper [17], at which time he added that the relational approach had "four main components":

1. Simplify to the greatest practical extent the types of data structure employed in the principal schema (or community view);

2. Introduce powerful operators to enable both programmers and nonprogrammers to store and retrieve target data *without having to "navigate" to the target;*

3. Introduce natural language (for example, English) with dialog support to permit effective interaction by casual (and possibly computer-naïve) users;

4. Express authorization and integrity constraints separately from the data structure (because they are liable to change).

"Discussions on the relational approach often become riveted on the first [of these components] to the neglect of the other three . . . To do justice to this approach, all four components must be considered as a package" [17].

Finally, in the paper [21] he presented on the occasion of his receiving the 1981 ACM Turing Award (richly deserved!) for his work on the relational model, Codd claims that truly relational systems can:

1. Put many database applications within the nonprogrammer's reach, where programmers were previously a necessity;

2. Increase the productivity of programmers on many (though not all) database applications

(slightly paraphrased).

It seems to me that these various lists of objectives and related matters together constitute a striking testimonial to Codd's huge achievement. I don't think anyone could seriously claim either (a) that any of the objectives is undesirable in itself or (b) that—with one possible exception—the relational model has failed in meeting them. The one possible exception is the one having to do with "the addition at a later time of inferential services in the commercial world." Providing such services is an issue that (so far as I know) is only just beginning to be seriously addressed in the DBMS marketplace. Nevertheless, there's every reason to believe that the relational model does indeed provide the right foundation for such services, owing in large part to its close relationship (noted in the previous chapter) to predicate logic.

SO WHAT *IS* THE RELATIONAL MODEL?

I pointed out in the previous chapter that, strangely enough, Codd apparently didn't even define the term "relational model" until 1979 [19]. Perhaps even more strangely, he didn't define the more general term "data model" until 1981! In a paper entitled "Data Models in Database Management" [20], he defines a data model to consist of a combination of three components:

1. A collection of data object types, which form the basic building blocks for any database that conforms to the model;

2. A collection of general integrity rules, which constrain the set of occurrences of those object types that can legally appear in any such database;

3. A collection of operators, which can be applied to such object occurrences for retrieval and other purposes

(somewhat paraphrased once again). By the way, note that *object* here is definitely not meant in the modern, rather restricted sense of "object orientation"!

The paper goes on to discuss what purpose data models in general, and the relational model in particular, are intended to serve, and offers evidence in support of the claim that—contrary to popular belief—the relational model was actually the *first* abstract data model to be defined. (As we saw in the previous chapter, the so-called hierarchic and network "models" were defined *after the fact* by a process of abstraction from already existing implementations. Though it's interesting to note in the light of this observation that Codd himself referred to "the hi-erarchic and network models" in his very first two pa-pers, dated 1969 and 1970 respectively.)

Be that as it may, the question arises: What then ex-actly *is* the relational model? If you've been following the discussions in Chapters 1–11 carefully, you'll have no-ticed that Codd's own definitions evolved somewhat throughout the 1970s and early 1980s. (Indeed, they've continued to change since that time, too.) One conse-quence of this fact is that critics have been able to accuse Codd in particular, and relational advocates in general, of "moving the goalposts" far too much. For example, Mike Stonebraker has written [59] that "one can think of four different versions" of the model:

- Version 1: Defined by the 1970 CACM paper [9]
- Version 2: Defined by the 1981 Turing Award paper [21]
- Version 3: Defined by Codd's 12 rules and scoring sys-tem [22]
- Version 4: Defined by Codd's book [23]

Perhaps because we're a trifle sensitive to such criti-cisms, Hugh Darwen and I have tried to provide, in *The Third Manifesto* [25,52], our own careful statement of what we believe the relational model is (or ought to be!). Indeed, we'd like the *Manifesto* to be seen in part as a de-finitive statement in this regard. I refer you to the docu-ment itself for the details; here just let me say that we see our contribution in this area as primarily one of dotting a few i's and crossing a few t's that Codd himself left un-dotted or uncrossed in his own original work. We most certainly do *not* want to be thought of as departing in any major respect from Codd's original vision; indeed, the whole of the *Manifesto* is very much as in the spirit of Codd's ideas and continues along the path that he originally laid down.

WHITHER THE RELATIONAL MODEL?

In Chapter 1, I said I expected database systems still to be based on Codd's relational foundation a hundred years from now. And I hope you can see, from what we've covered in preceding chapters, why I believe such a thing. The relational approach really is rock solid, owing (once again) to its basis in mathematics and predicate logic. (Of course, I don't mean to suggest that the model solves all known problems and will never need any extensions; as we saw in the previous chapter, extensions are certainly possible and sometimes desirable. I just mean, to repeat, that the *foundation* is solid.)

I'd like to conclude by summarizing an argument that Codd himself presented (under the heading "Whither Database Management?") in the Great Debate paper [17], having to do with alternative possibilities for the future development of database: systems. We start by assuming we're given the simplest possible programmer-oriented interface to the database: namely, a record-at-a-time interface, with operators like "get first," "get next," and so on. Then:

1. If we add high-level operators (join and so forth), we get *automatic navigation*—meaning that even nonprogrammers can get to their targets unaided.

2. Alternatively, if we don't add such operators but do add new data structures, such as links, then *manual navigation* becomes a necessity—meaning that programmers become indispensable in the task of helping end users get to their targets.

3. And if we add both operators and structure, then we get *needless complexity*—meaning that many more decisions have to be made by both programmers and the database administrator (without, I might add, any good guidelines as to how to make those decisions).

The conclusion is surely obvious.

Appendix A

A Definition of the Relational Model

For purposes of reference, we offer the following formal definition (taken from reference [49]) of the relational model. The definition is deliberately much more abstract than any of those given in the body of this book. See either reference [49] or reference [52] for further explanation.

Briefly, the relational model consists of the following five components:

1. An open-ended collection of **scalar types** (including in particular the type *boolean* or *truth value*);
2. A **relation type generator** and an intended interpretation for relations of types generated thereby;
3. Facilities for defining **relation variables** of such generated relation types;
4. A **relational assignment** operation for assigning relation values to such relation variables;
5. An open-ended collection of generic **relational operators** for deriving relation values from other relation values.

We offer the following additional commentary on these five components:

1. The scalar types can be system- or user-defined, in general; thus, a means must be available for users to define their own types (this requirement is implied, partly, by the fact that the set of types is "open-ended"). A means must therefore also be available for users to define their own operators, since types without operators are useless. The only *required* system-defined type is type *boolean* (the most fundamental type of all), but a real system will surely support integers, strings, etc., as builtin types as well.

2. The relation type generator allows users to define their own relation types. The "intended interpretation" for a given relation (of a given relation type) is the corresponding *predicate* (see reference [49] or reference [52]).

3. Facilities for defining relation variables *must* be available (of course). Relation variables are the *only* variables allowed inside a relational database.

4. Variables are updatable by definition; hence, every kind of variable is subject to *assignment,* and relation variables are no exception. INSERT, UPDATE, and DELETE shorthands are legal and indeed useful, but strictly speaking they *are* only shorthands.

5. The "generic operators" are the operators that make up the relational algebra, and they are therefore builtin (though there is no inherent reason why users should not be able to define additional ones). They are "generic" because they apply to all possible relations, loosely speaking.

Appendix B

References and Bibliography

1. A. V. Aho, C. Beeri, and J. D. Ullman: "The Theory of Joins in Relational Databases," *ACM Transactions on Database Systems 4,* No. 3 (September 1979). First published in Proc. 19th IEEE Symp. on Foundations of Computer Science (October 1977).

2. M. M. Astrahan *et al.*: "System R: Relational Approach to Database Management," *ACM Transactions on Database Systems 1,* No. 2 (June 1976).

3. Colin J. Bell: "A Relational Model for Information Retrieval and the Processing of Linguistic Data," IBM Research Report RC1705 (November 3rd, 1966).

4. D. Bjørner, E. F. Codd, K. L. Deckert, and I. L. Traiger: "The GAMMA-0 *N*-ary Relational Data Base Interface: Specifications of Objects and Operations," IBM Research Report RJ1200 (April 11th, 1973).

5. Peter Pin-Shan Chen: "The Entity-Relationship Model—Toward a Unified View of Data," *ACM Transactions on Database Systems 1,* No. 1 (March 1976). Republished in Michael Stonebraker (ed.): *Readings in Database Systems* (2nd edition). San Mateo, Calif.: Morgan Kaufmann (1994).

6. E. F. Codd *et al.*: "Multiprogramming STRETCH: Feasibility Considerations," *CACM 2,* No. 11 (November 1959); E. F. Codd: "Multiprogram Scheduling" (in two parts), *CACM 3,* Nos. 6 and 7 (June/July 1960).

7. E. F. Codd: "Derivability, Redundancy, and Consistency of Relations Stored in Large Data Banks," IBM Research Report RJ599 (August 19th, 1969).

8. E. F. Codd: "Notes on a Data Sublanguage," IBM internal memo (January 19th, 1970).

143

9. E. F. Codd: "A Relational Model of Data for Large Shared Data Banks," *CACM 13*, No. 6 (June 1970). Republished in *Milestones of Research—Selected Papers 1958–1982 (CACM 25th Anniversary Issue), CACM 26*, No. 1 (January 1983).

10. E. F. Codd: "The Second and Third Normal Forms for the Relational Model," IBM technical memo (October 6th, 1970).

11. E. F. Codd: "A Data Base Sublanguage Founded on the Relational Calculus," IBM Research Report RJ893 (July 26th, 1971). Republished in Proc. 1971 ACM SIGFIDET Workshop on Data Description, Access and Control, San Diego, Calif. (November 1971).

12. E. F. Codd: "Further Normalization of the Data Base Relational Model" (presented at Courant Computer Science Symposia Series 6, "Data Base Systems," New York City, N.Y., May 24th–25th, 1971). IBM Research Report RJ909 (August 31st, 1971). Republished in Randall J. Rustin (ed.), *Data Base Systems: Courant Computer Science Symposia Series 6*. Englewood Cliffs, N.J.: Prentice-Hall (1972).

13. E. F. Codd: "Normalized Data Base Structure: A Brief Tutorial," Proc. 1971 ACM SIGFIDET Workshop on Data Description, Access, and Control, San Diego, Calif. (November 11th–12th, 1971).

14. E. F. Codd: Private communication (March 14th, 1972).

15. E. F. Codd: "Relational Completeness of Data Base Sublanguages" (presented at Courant Computer Science Symposia Series 6, "Data Base Systems," New York City, N.Y., May 24th–25th, 1971). IBM Research Report RJ987 (March 6th, 1972). Republished in Randall J. Rustin (ed.), *Data Base Systems: Courant Computer Science Symposia Series 6*. Englewood Cliffs, N.J.: Prentice-Hall (1972).

16. E. F. Codd: "Seven Steps to Rendezvous with the Casual User," IBM Research Report RJ1333 (January 7th, 1974). Republished in J. W. Klimbie and K. L. Koffeman (eds.), *Data Base Management*, Proc. IFIP TC-2 Working Conference on Data Base Management. New York, N.Y.: North-Holland (1974).

17. E. F. Codd and C. J. Date: "Interactive Support for Nonprogrammers: The Relational and Network Approaches," IBM Research Report RJ1400 (June 6th, 1974). Republished in Randall J. Rustin (ed.), Proc. ACM SIGMOD Workshop on Data Description, Access, and Control, Vol. II, Ann Arbor, Michigan (May 1974) and in

C. J. Date, *Relational Database: Selected Writings*. Reading, Mass.: Addison-Wesley (1986). See also E. F. Codd: "The Significance of the SQL/Data System Announcement," IBM Report (January 30th, 1981).

18. E. F. Codd: "Recent Investigations into Relational Data Base Systems," IBM Research Report RJ1385 (April 23rd, 1974). Republished in Proc. 1974 Congress (Stockholm, Sweden, 1974). New York, N.Y.: North-Holland (1974).

19. E. F. Codd: "Extending the Database Relational Model to Capture More Meaning," IBM Research Report RJ2599 (August 6th, 1979). Republished in *ACM Transactions on Database Systems 4*, No. 4 (December 1979).

20. E. F. Codd: "Data Models in Database Management," in Michael L. Brodie and Stephen N. Zilles (eds.), Proc. Workshop on Data Abstraction, Databases, and Conceptual Modelling, Pingree Park, Colo. (June 1980): Joint Issue, *ACM SIGART Newsletter* No. 74 (January 1981); *ACM SIGMOD Record 11*, No. 2 (February 1981); *ACM SIGPLAN Notices 16*, No. 1 (January 1981).

21. E. F. Codd: "Relational Database: A Practical Foundation for Productivity," IBM Research Report RJ3339 (Decmber 21st, 1981). Republished in *CACM 25*, No. 2 (February 1982).

22. E. F. Codd: "Is Your DBMS Really Relational?" and "Does Your DBMS Run By The Rules?", *Computerworld* (October 14th, 1985; October 21st, 1985).

23. E. F. Codd: *The Relational Model For Database Management Version 2*. Reading, Mass.: Addison-Wesley (1990).

24. Hugh Darwen: "Relation-Valued Attributes; *or*, Will the Real First Normal Form Please Stand Up?", in C. J. Date and Hugh Darwen, *Relational Database Writings 1989-1991*. Reading, Mass.: Addison-Wesley (1992).

25. Hugh Darwen and C. J. Date: "The Third Manifesto," *ACM SIGMOD Record 24*, No. 1 (March 1995).

26. C. J. Date: "An Introduction to the Unified Database Language (UDL)," Proc. 6th International Conference on Very Large Data Bases, Montreal, Canada (September/October 1980). Republished (in considerably revised form) in C. J. Date, *Relational Database: Selected Writings*, Addison-Wesley (1986).

27. C. J. Date: "A Critique of the SQL Database Language," *ACM SIGMOD Record 14,* No. 3 (November 1984). Republished in C. J. Date, *Relational Database: Selected Writings.* Reading, Mass.: Addison-Wesley (1986).

28. C. J. Date: *A Guide to INGRES.* Reading, Mass.: Addison-Wesley (1987).

29. C. J. Date: "Why Relational?", in C. J. Date, *Relational Database Writings 1985–1989.* Reading, Mass.: Addison-Wesley (1990).

30. C. J. Date: "Support for the Conceptual Schema: The Relational and Network Approaches," in C. J. Date, *Relational Database Writings 1985–1989.* Reading, Mass.: Addison-Wesley (1990).

31. C. J. Date: "A Note on the Relational Calculus," *ACM SIGMOD Record 18,* No. 4 (December 1989). Republished as "An Anomaly in Codd's Reduction Algorithm" in C. J. Date and Hugh Darwen, *Relational Database Writings 1989–1991.* Reading, Mass.: Addison-Wesley (1992).

32. C. J. Date: "The Importance of Closure," in C. J. Date, *Relational Database Writings 1991–1994.* Reading, Mass.: Addison-Wesley (1995).

33. C. J. Date: "Tables with No Columns," in C. J. Date, *Relational Database Writings 1991–1994.* Reading, Mass.: Addison-Wesley (1995).

34. C. J. Date: "Expression Transformation" (in two parts), in C. J. Date, *Relational Database Writings 1991–1994.* Reading, Mass.: Addison-Wesley (1995).

35. C. J. Date: "The Primacy of Primary Keys: An Investigation," *InfoDB 7,* No. 3 ("Summer" 1993—published November 1993). Republished in C. J. Date, *Relational Database Writings 1991–1994.* Reading, Mass.: Addison-Wesley (1995).

36. C. J. Date: "Divide—and Conquer?", in C. J. Date, *Relational Database Writings 1991–1994.* Reading, Mass.: Addison-Wesley (1995).

37. C. J. Date: "Relational Comparisons," in C. J. Date, *Relational Database Writings 1991–1994.* Reading, Mass.: Addison-Wesley (1995).

38. C. J. Date: "Many Happy Returns!", in C. J. Date, *Relational Database Writings 1991–1994.* Reading, Mass.: Addison-Wesley (1995).

39. C. J. Date: "Essentiality," in C. J. Date, *Relational Database Writings 1991–1994*. Reading, Mass.: Addison-Wesley (1995).

40. C. J. Date: "The Extended Relational Model RM/T," in C. J. Date, *Relational Database Writings 1991–1994*. Reading, Mass.: Addison-Wesley (1995).

41. C. J. Date: "It's All Relations!", in C. J. Date, Hugh Darwen, and David McGoveran: *Relational Database Writings 1994–1997*. Reading, Mass.: Addison-Wesley (1998).

42. C. J. Date: "Nested Relations" (in two parts), in C. J. Date, Hugh Darwen, and David McGoveran: *Relational Database Writings 1994–1997*. Reading, Mass.: Addison-Wesley (1998).

43. C. J. Date: "Quota Queries" (in three parts), in C. J. Date, Hugh Darwen, and David McGoveran: *Relational Database Writings 1994–1997*. Reading, Mass.: Addison-Wesley (1998).

44. C. J. Date: "The Final Normal Form!" (Part 2), *Database Programming & Design 11,* No. 2 (February 1998).

45. C. J. Date: "Normalization Is No Panacea," *Database Programming & Design 11,* No. 4 (April 1998).

46. C. J. Date: "The Birth of the Relational Model" (Part 3), *Intelligent Enterprise 1,* No. 3 (December 1998), online at *www.intelligententerprise.com;* also in *Intelligent Enterprise 1,* No. 4 (December 15th, 1998). Chapter 3 of the present book.

47. C. J. Date: "Codd's Relational Algebra," *Intelligent Enterprise 2,* No. 1 (January 5th, 1999), online at *www.intelligententerprise.com*. Chapter 4 of the present book.

48. C. J. Date: "Don't Mix Pointers and Relations!" and "Don't Mix Pointers and Relations—*Please!*", in C. J. Date, Hugh Darwen, and David McGoveran: *Relational Database Writings 1994–1997*. Reading, Mass.: Addison-Wesley (1998).

49. C. J. Date: *An Introduction to Database Systems* (7th edition). Reading, Mass.: Addison-Wesley (2000). *Note:* The first edition of this book (referenced in Chapter 1 of the present book) had a copyright date of 1975. The third edition (referenced in Chapter 8) had a copyright date of 1981.

50. C. J. Date and E. F. Codd: "The Relational and Network Approaches: Comparison of the Application Programming Interfaces," IBM Research Report RJ1401 (June 6th, 1974). Republished in Randall J. Rustin (ed.), Proc. ACM SIGMOD

Workshop on Data Description, Access, and Control, Vol. II, Ann
Arbor, Michigan (May 1974) and in C. J. Date, *Relational Database: Selected Writings*. Reading, Mass.: Addison-Wesley (1986).

51. C. J. Date and Hugh Darwen: *A Guide to the SQL Standard* (4th
edition). Reading, Mass.: Addison-Wesley (1997).

52. C. J. Date and Hugh Darwen: *Foundation for Object/Relational
Databases: The Third Manifesto*. Reading, Mass.: Addison-Wesley
(1998). A second edition of this book, under the revised title *Foundation for Future Database Systems: The Third Manifesto,* is due
to appear concurrently with the present book.

53. Ronald Fagin: "Normal Forms and Relational Database Operators," Proc. 1979 ACM SIGMOD International Conference on
Management of Data, Boston, Mass. (May/June 1979).

54. I. J. Heath: "Unacceptable File Operations in a Relational Database," Proc. 1971 ACM SIGFIDET Workshop on Data Description,
Access, and Control, San Diego, Calif. (November 11th–12th, 1971).

55. G. D. Held, M. R. Stonebraker, and E. Wong: "INGRES—A Relational Data Base System," Proc. NCC *44,* Anaheim, Calif. Mont-
vale, N.J.: AFIPS Press (May 1975).

56. James Martin: "Semantic Disintegrity in Relational Operations,"
Chapter 18 of *Fourth-Generation Languages Volume I: Principles*.
Englewood Cliffs, N.J.: Prentice-Hall (1985).

57. Frank P. Palermo: "A Data Base Search Problem," IBM Research
Report RJ1072 (July 27th, 1972). Republished in Julius T. Tou
(ed.), *Information Systems: COINS IV*. New York, N.Y.: Plenum
Press (1974).

58. Jorma Rissanen: "Independent Components of Relations," *ACM
Transactions on Database Systems 2,* No. 4 (December 1977).

59. Michael Stonebraker: Introduction to Chapter 1 ("The Roots"),
Readings in Database Systems (2nd edition). San Mateo, Calif.:
Morgan Kaufmann (1994).

60. Jeffrey D. Ullman: *Principles of Database and Knowledge-Base
Systems: Volume I*. Rockville, Maryland: Computer Science Press
(1988).

61. Carlo Zaniolo: "A New Normal Form for the Design of Relational
Database Schemata," *ACM Transactions on Database Systems 7,*
No. 3 (September 1982).

Index

θ-join, *see* join
θ-restriction, *see* restriction
1NF, *see* first normal form
2NF, *see* second normal form
3NF, *see* third normal form
5NF, *see* fifth normal form

abstract data type, 68, 122
access language features, 14–15
access path dependence, 30
active domain, 9
Adleman, L., 3
ADT, *see* abstract data type
aggregate function, 71
Aho, Alfred V., 143
algebra, 42–43
  relational, *see* relational algebra
ALPHA, 65ff
alpha expression, 53–54
alternate key, 93
anomaly (insert/update/delete), 93, 103
  caused by redundancy, 104
assignment (relational), *see* relational assignment
association, 129
Astrahan, Morton M., 143
atomicity of values, 31, 33, 38
attribute, 8
attribute migration, 77–78, 104
automatic navigation, 139

Bachman, Charles W., 105
bag, 71
BCNF, *see* Boyce/Codd normal form
Beeri, Catriel, 143
Bell, Colin J., 143
Bjørner, Dines, 143
bound variable, *see* free variable
Boyce, Raymond F., 101

Boyce/Codd normal form, 101–102

calculus, 52
  relational, *see* relational calculus
candidate key, 11, 92
Cartesian product, 45
  expanded, 45
cascade delete, *see* referential action
catalog, 68, 76–77
  RM/T, 128
characteristic, 128–129
Chen, Peter Pin-Shan, 143
China, 86
closed world interpretation, 125–126
closure, *see* relational algebra
CODASYL, 81, 105ff
CODASYL set, 111
  see also link
Codd, Edgar F., *passim*
  summary of contributions, 5–6, 135
Codd's reduction algorithm, 59–60
column, 8
comparison (relational), *see* relational comparison
composition, 17
  natural, 17
connection trap, 35

Darwen, Hugh, 33, 67, 88, 121, 137, 145, 148
data bank, 10
data independence
  logical, 22, 29, 78
  physical, 28, 29
data model, 136
data sublanguage, 14
Data Sublanguage ALPHA, *see* ALPHA
database, 10

149